A Phenomenology of Racism in Counselling and Psychotherapy

I0095098

Using the experiential frameworks of phenomenology and existentialism, *A Phenomenology of Racism in Counselling and Psychotherapy* unveils the layers of relational intersectional racism which are embedded within our culture, and its many forms.

This book recognises that race in its origins was a social system built out of white European supremacy which held within itself both class and patriarchal structures. It examines the extensive layers of societally embedded racism from those more obvious and fuelled by hate, to the covert but equally as psychologically destructive, to that which then becomes more deeply internalised by those seen as the racialised other. Theoretical explorations of how our early life experiences build our relational identity around race and the long-term internalised impacts of racism, be they neurological, psychological, or trauma-based, sit central to this exploration. Utilising personal and case material, Turner then details how working creatively with dreams and other means of accessing the unconscious can be essential pathways for counsellors, psychotherapists, and psychologists, as we assist our clients (and ourselves) in working through the pain of the internalisations of racist experiences.

This unique text is designed to assist professionals across the helping professions in understanding and working more wholly and effectively with the constructs of race and experiences of racism.

Dr Dwight Turner is an activist, a writer, and public speaker on issues of race, difference, and intersectionality in counselling and psychotherapy. A Psychotherapist, Supervisor, Workshop Facilitator, and Conference Presenter in Private Practice, he is also currently the Course Leader in Humanistic Counselling at the University of Brighton. His books include *Decolonizing Counselling and Psychotherapy* (2025), *The Psychology of Supremacy* (2023), and *Intersections of Privilege and Otherness in Counselling and Psychotherapy* (2021).

A Phenomenology of Racism in Counselling and Psychotherapy

Dwight Turner

Routledge
Taylor & Francis Group

LONDON AND NEW YORK

Designed cover image: Getty Images

First published 2026
by Routledge
4 Park Square, Milton Park, Abingdon, Oxon OX14 4RN

and by Routledge
605 Third Avenue, New York, NY 10158

Routledge is an imprint of the Taylor & Francis Group, an informa business

British Library Cataloguing-in-Publication Data
A catalogue record for this book is available from the British Library

ISBN: 978-1-032-83342-2 hbk)
ISBN: 978-1-032-83340-8 (pbk)
ISBN: 978-1-003-50885-4 (ebk)

DOI: 10.4324/9781003508854

Typeset in Times New Roman
by KnowledgeWorks Global Ltd.

Contents

Acknowledgements   *vi*
Preface   *vii*

1 Introduction   1

2 The Phenomenology of Racism   18

3 The Trauma of Racism   42

4 The Somatising of Racism   68

5 The Privilege of Vulnerability versus the Invincibility
  of Suffering   90

6 Conclusion   120

Index   *128*

Acknowledgements

There is a pain in the loneliness in experiences of racism which echoes the pain in the solitude utilised by authors in any writing process.

That is one of the reasons why writing about this subject is so incredibly difficult.

To do so, one has to go back into both spaces; to relive the oft traumatic wounds of racialised loneliness, whilst delving deep to excavate the creativity embedded within the writer's solitude as one makes sense of said pain.

So, as I reemerge at the end of this process, as I resurface, bruised, battered, and scarred (but hard), this book is simply for me.

It's done!

Preface

I think I need to begin this book with some personal reasons as to why this is one of my most important works within counselling and psychotherapy.

So here goes …

Every book submitted to a publisher has to go through a review process, and I have been lucky that my editor at Routledge has regularly found some very encouraging people to review my work.

In an early review of this book though, one of the reviewers stated that although this book was about racism, they were worried about my revealing so much of myself in these pages. Their comments, which I took with the kindness I believe they held within them, hinted at the possible backlash which would/could/might come my way were I to speak my own truth about racism. The aim was not to silence me, but was I believe borne out of a genuine concern for my wellbeing as this is a very difficult thing to do, this project. The challenge of self-care was there and is something I would be wise to listen to as this text finds its audience (and would advise readers to follow as well). Yet, conversely, when I sat down and thought about the importance of this book, its importance and its relevance to the current cultural climate, I realised that writing a phenomenological text about racism could only work if I were willing to tell my own and others' stories on these pages.

So here goes…

A story out of the collective to begin with. In August 2024 in Southport, in the United Kingdom, three young children, aged between six and nine, were killed as they attended a Taylor Swift-themed dance class, with another ten children and adults being seriously injured (Sherlock, 2024). This horrific event, committed by a Christian man from Cardiff in Wales, quite rightly led to a collective outpouring of sadness and compassion across the country. The additional horrors begun when, through the use of social media to spread misinformation and lies, the Far Right blamed immigrants and Muslims in the United Kingdom for this atrocity, leading to several nights of riots in cities across the country (Mackintosh, 2024).

The impact upon racialised communities across the country though was immense. We watched as Eastern European taxi drivers were pulled from their cars and beaten, as Muslim women had their hijabs pulled off in public, as Filipino nurses were shouted at and abused as they walked to work, and as refugees were forced to flee their abodes as they were set alight, all by rioters and thugs claiming they wanted to take their country back.

Then something interesting happened. Anti-Fascist, and anti-racist protest sprung up across the United Kingdom. From Belfast, to Bristol, to Birmingham. From Walthamstow, to Sunderland, to Brighton. Tens of thousands of people from all cultures, be their Romany, Muslim, Jewish, Christian, or White British, came out to support the racialised other. They marched, they sang, they stood in silent solidarity with all the groups targeted by the cult of misinformation unleashed by the Far Right (Manning & Moench, 2024). The collective in support of each other in opposition to those who would marginalise and abuse them.

I want to follow this up though with a personal story.

On 12th December 2018, whilst on my way home from a pre-Christmas night out in Brighton, as I disembarked at Eastbourne Station, a strange, painful incident occurred. As I walked along the platform towards the ticket barriers, gently humming to myself, a woman, white, dark haired, slightly drunk, walked towards me and shouted at me,

'What's up my nigger?'

Immediately torn from my post night out reverie, I remember standing there stunned by the fact that this person, who I had never met, who I didn't know, had chosen to say something so hard, so cold, to someone she had herself never met and didn't know. As the woman walked past me though, I turned back and shouted at her. The woman stopped and turned around. I angrily told her that I didn't like what she had said and told her to apologise. The woman did so. She said sorry. So, I let it go, and then began to walk away.

'What's up my nigger?!' the woman said again, whispering under her breadth, just enough for several other passengers to hear.

Really angry now, I turned around and wanted to confront her. But the woman had run onto the waiting train. Following her onto the train, the woman then yelled at me, shouting that she had a right to say what she wanted. Pointing at me, yelling, and defiantly standing her ground. In the end, all I did was to then take her picture before I left the train just as a guard appeared. I reported the incident to him. He took down my details, and the whole issue was passed on to the British Transport Police.

Sadly, or unsurprisingly, a few weeks after this case, I received a call from the police stating that they had not found the person involved and that they were taking the case no further. I do not recall if any support was offered to myself (although I suspect it wasn't). I was then just left on my own. With my story, painful coping mechanisms, and with my anger.

I find it strange that so many people still in the current era deny the existence of racism. When you consider the horrors of the summer of 2024, and just how afraid so many persons of racialised difference were in the wake of the Far Right riots, to advocate that something so centrally driven, and which impacts so many disparate groups, that it doesn't exist, plays into one of the central tenets of racism: that of silencing the other.

This is something I myself have endured. For example, when I tell some people about Eastbourne Incident XXXX of 12/12/18, quite often though, my statement, my story, is then filtered through rationalised systemic excuses such as: if this woman was drunk, then she wouldn't have known what she was doing? Or am I really sure that is what happened? Or that I am just making it up for attention (and yes, I have heard all of these)? The fact that later that night I barely slept, that I overate the following day, that I felt the deep wellspring of pain, of sadness, and of anger as I replayed everything from what I would have done and said differently, to how much I wanted to disassemble that woman; none of these things were ever expressed to anyone other than my therapist. Until now.

When I was revisiting these episodes, scanning the numerous stories on social media, and reading my old journals whilst researching narratives for this book, I somehow found myself returning to the work of the civil rights activist, orator and writer James Baldwin. One particular story and quote of his stood out. In 1963, when he was being interviewed by a reporter from *Life Magazine*. During the interview, Baldwin stated that:

> You think your pain and your heartbreak are unprecedented in the history of the world, but then you read. It was Dostoevsky and Dickens who taught me that the things that tormented me most were the very things that connected to me with all the people who were alive, or who ever had been alive. Only if we face these open wounds in ourselves can we understand them in other people.
>
> (Iyengar, 2022, p. 1)

Racism, much like the other isms and phobias of hate, holds within it two things. First of all is the siloing effect; that sense that what has just happened to oneself, that microaggression of being subtly put down, or the more overt aggressions of being called a racial slur, only happens to oneself. Racism isolates us in its attack on our core, taking the victim to a place where they themselves also forget the range of intersectional identities they might hold. Secondly, racism silences the other. In its attack on the humanity of the racialised other there comes deeply embedded within it a sense that one's voice has been taken, nay stolen, from the throat chakras which might have borne it.

Systemic racism is divisive because the controlling defining force of systemic whiteness needs it to be. In its creation of splits racism divides groups, it divides communities, it divides families, it divides the individual. Racism defies and disempowers, but perhaps more importantly for this phenomenological exploration, racism shames and it silences.

Baldwin's words therefore reconnected me to these example(s) and encouraged me to redouble my efforts in gleaning the narratives of so many others who have suffered this kind of abuse. Not so much out of a need to bare one's soul narcissistically, but more out of a need to build connection. To create a lattice work of solace and understanding around a topic area which by its very nature is both silencing and isolating, in its covert and overt aggressions.

This connection, this patchwork of phenomenological perspectives on something so insidious also meets another need. As shown in the outpouring of love and support from so many in the days following the initial riots of the Summer of 2024, community connection is self-care. When we break bread with our families and/or friends we get nourishment – this is self-care. When we march with compatriots in the name of some morally driven protest, this is self-care. When we sit with ourselves on retreat, and tune into the unconscious spaces of our own shadow, this is self-care. Self-care, to borrow from Audre Lorde, is a revolutionary act (Lorde, 1984). The meeting of mutual minds, of similar experiences, often holds within it the mirroring of compassion, as our companion holds with us the pain of racialised marginalisation, whilst returning to us the humanity stolen from us by the racialised hatred of the subject.

That is the importance of a book like this one. The fact that I, that we, that so many of us have stories to tell about racism. That pushing past the internalised voice of supremacy which silences us into compliance, that working through the physical adaptations which keep the racialised other performative, that our stories when told re-humanise us. They bring us back to life, escaping the melancholic morass which endurances of racism force us into. So, when I tell these stories, my participants as well as my own, it is as much about the breaking of said spell as it is about acknowledging and severing the unconscious silencing illusion of systemic whiteness.

So, as the reader of this tome scans these phenomenological perspectives, and as they delve into their own intersectionally driven experience of racism, I would advise them to do something of the same as part of their self-care. Speak up. Find a space with like-minded people or do what you need to alone with your deeper self. Seek out whatever you need to in order to support yourself as the traumatic echoes from the experiences of your own racialised identities sprint to the surface to be known once again.

Just as I have done by writing this book, and as I will continue to do as people talk as me about its content.

So here goes …

References

Iyengar, S. (2022). *Taking a Page from Baldwin: Book-Reading as a Violence-Coping and Prevention Strategy*. National Endowment for the Arts. www.arts.gov/stories/blog/2022/taking-page-baldwin-book-reading-violence-coping-and-prevention-strategy#:~:text=In 1963%2C James Baldwin told a LIFE magazine,were alive%2C or who ever had been alive.

Lorde, A. (1984). *Sister outsider*. Crossing Press Limited.

Mackintosh, T. (2024). *New rioting across UK cities as arrests multiply*. BBC News Online. www.bbc.co.uk/news/articles/cn5rr1433k3o

Manning, L., & Moench, M. (2024). *Anti-racism protesters rally after week of riots*. BBC News Online. www.bbc.co.uk/news/articles/czxlgwl28gyo

Sherlock, G. (2024). *A town in mourning – but its spirit is not broken*. BBC News Online. www.bbc.co.uk/news/articles/c1epp863wnlo

Chapter 1

Introduction

When I was in my mid-thirties, I was travelling through Malaysia on a holi-day. This was a period of my life when I was travelling on my own and a period of my life where I was on the whole staying away from relationships. I had completed my training to become a psychotherapist and experiential training which had taken an awful lot out of myself during this period, and I needed a bit of time to put myself back together, to find myself, and to work out who I really was.

Whilst on my travels, I met a group of three British women. We introduced ourselves, we talked, we got on well and for some reason we decided to go out to a nightclub in Kuala Lumpur. Whilst at said nightclub, one of the women and I became quite friendly. We spent a fair amount of time together, embraced, kissed, but when we got back to the hotel later on, although she suggested that I come back to her room, I actually turned her down because like I said I was staying outside of relationships. We briefly spoke the next day, some nice platitudes over breakfast, how nice it was to spend time with each other, that sort of thing, and there was a loose promise that when we were both back in the United Kingdom we would keep in touch.

Perhaps ten days or two weeks later, I rang this woman with a view to per-haps meeting up. During our conversation, I suggested as much. My sug-gestion though led to the revelation that this woman did not want to see me again, not because she was not interested as such, but because in her words,

'I would never be seen out with a Black person in England. I just felt it would be a good thing for us to maybe sleep together so I could try out what it was like to be with a Black man.'

The conversation ended not long after that and of course I never spoke to or saw this person again.

The reason I lead this volume with that particular story is because this experience of racism is not uncommon for persons who hold some sort of racialised identity. The idea that this woman saw me only as a Black man, only as a black cock, and

DOI: 10.4324/9781003508854-1

only as the other, an object to be played around with, is a fairly common experience when we factor in that we all have a racialised identity.

The difficult part about an experience of racism though, is that it is often very hard to talk about like any other form of abuse. There is something within the experience of being racially picked out, picked on, undermined, spoken over, where one loses one's own sense of who they are and also loses one's own voice. The importance therefore of leading this text with a story such as this is to actually lay the groundwork for what will happen throughout this tome, as I start to explore and investigate just what racism actually is from a phenomenological perspective.

The second thing to recognise when exploring a topic of racialised oppression is that the subject, or those who identify as white, or superior, or whatever term they choose to use, become allies to the cause of those who have been marginalised and left out and put to one side, giving back the voice to the racialised other. There have been numerous texts produced over the past few years which have attempted to do this, texts which speak of the experience of being not just the other but the racialised other and their experiences of racism (Ellis, 2021; Kinouani, 2021). These works show how important it is to bring awareness and understanding and to provide a voice for those who have been put to one side and not seen previously. This holds echoes from other communities as well, such as the brilliant Queering Psychotherapy which provides a narrative and a voice from an LGBTQ+ perspective and other books which have done the same from a disability standpoint or from even within feminist discourses (Barnes, 2016; Gilligan, 1995; Various, 2022).

The voice is massively important here and I do not just mean the spoken word, I mean the written word on a piece of paper, or on an electronic reading device. I mean the song that is sung as a form of hope when one has experienced racism, such as Sam Cook's 'A Change is Gonna Come', or Eminem's song 'Untouchable', both of which speak of white supremacy (Cooke, 2016; Eminem, 2017). This can come up in forms of artwork such as Basquiat and others whose work is infused with their racialised identity (Clement, 2014). The voice and how we express the pain of what it is to be a person of racial difference, of colour, to be black, to be BAME, becomes the first stage in actually unveiling our experience for those who might empathise with us.

When George Floyd was murdered in May 2020 during the early days of a global pandemic, when so many of us were sat at home under lockdowns, one of the most interesting facets of that whole experience with hindsight was how global the reach of his death was (Various, 2020). The fact that this singular man, this father to five children was seen not just as a man who had lost his life under the knee of police officers in Minneapolis, but rather as a man who may have in the past committed certain crimes and therefore did not deserve to be seen as a human being. The intersecting layers of racism which sat on both sides of this debate around the death of a man, of a human being, were fascinating to behold. Yet, what they did do for a good number of people is prompt and spark elements of frustration, sadness, and anger in the many peoples of racial difference across the world, who had previously seen themselves as the other and therefore as without agency, without a voice, without a way of having their experience(s) known (Various, 2021b). This second example of racism, from my client work, speaks of the pain of not having a voice, together with this need for a voice in these discussions:

> Clara was a client of mine who I had worked with for a number of years and whose original presenting issue was more about difficult childhood issues than anything else. Being from an Afro-Caribbean background she had chosen to seek out Black therapists to work with throughout her therapeutic journey and I was the latest one of these. Our work changed dramatically with George Floyd's murder. Clara was employed at the time by a major company in London. She was the only woman of colour in her whole department so, when George Floyd's life was so savagely stolen from him on national television, and on social media time and time again, Clara spoke to her manager about their need for some means, some way, some form of diversity training within the department. This was prompted very much by some of the comments that her colleagues were making about George Floyd's murder, that he was just a criminal, that he deserved to lose his life, that suggested he was not really a human being.
>
> The manager said all the right things, yes, they would do some training; yes, they would take this into consideration; yes, what happened was awful. Yet nothing changed. What Clara realised, and what we discussed, was that within the organisation, although there were legal reasons and legal routes that she could follow in order to encourage, inveigle, or even force said department to look at the biases and the racism that sits within it, the lack of willingness of her own manager to do so meant that it would be a bit like pushing a rock up a hill.
>
> The second part to it though, for Clara, was the reason she then left the organisation. She no longer felt safe. This was important because in our work we had realised that what safety meant in that organisation was that she did not bring her Blackness to work. Her Blackness was not seen in her employment. She hid very much of who she was. She played out the double consciousness of Du Bois' work (1903). She wore the adaptation that Maya Angelou speaks about in her writings. She became that which was necessary to fit in and to play the role. She code switched is another word that I could use here. But when all of that became too much, and when she cried out for support from her colleagues because she was in pain at seeing the death of one of her race, what she realised was that support was not going to be there.
>
> It was heartbreaking for myself, as a therapist, and as a therapist of colour, to watch Clara realise what she had done to herself in order to fit into white environments and it became her own choice to then ultimately leave and find work elsewhere, where she felt safer and, as importantly, more supported.

This example, this story of the experience of not just overt but more subtle forms of racism post the death of George Floyd and during the pandemic was something that

I heard a lot more of in my work. A number of colleagues that I have had have left organisations where they were the only person of difference, of colour, not necessarily just of race, because for varying reasons their safety was not considered by said organisation.

Race and racism, this intertwined double-headed hydra, causes so much distress for those who are on the wrong side of the racialised divide. We only have to look at history, the marginalisation, and the annihilation, or should I say annihilations plural, of huge groups of people, communities, racialised others, based around the fact that they have been seen as the other. World wars, colonial atrocities, mass murders across Africa, Asia, Europe, are often built around one race being deemed as less than an other. So, in choosing to write a book like this, bringing a focus to race and racism, and bringing a voice to those who have not been given said voice, then becomes imperative in building back a level of trust and empathy for the racialised other that has not been there before.

Black Orpheus redux

In its original form, *Black Orpheus* was written by John Paul Sartre (1948) as the preface to the *Anthologie des la Nuvelle Poesie Negre et Malgache de Langue Française*, which was a book of poetry edited by Leopold Sedar Senghor (Julaud, 2019). This preface, which has subsequently been published as its own sort of text under the title of *Black Orpheus*, did a few things for the original text. It lent credence to the books or poetry that it was related to, but what it also did is it took the voice of the ally to then lift and promote the voices of the racialised other. This is an important facet here and although I am not necessarily certain that Sartre meant to play the role of the ally, what I do think it does for my text is it highlights the binary nature of the recovery from racism.

Race at its core is a dual relational construct. What I mean here is that systemic whiteness identifies itself by what it is and what it is not and it ascribes what it is not to Blackness, or the racialised other. In a way, this is no different to the social construction of gender, whereby what it is to be a man was defined by men and what it was not to be a man was ascribed towards women and is no different from the construct of class as well, where the ways of being as somebody from the upper classes were ascribed and have been developed over a period of time by those from the upper classes who were normally also male and also white, and anything that was seen as not worthy of the upper classes was passed down to the working classes accordingly (Aosved et al., 2009; Beauvoir, 2010; Turner, 2018, 2023).

Social constructions are therefore binary in notion (Various, 2019). They are also behavioural, and they evolve over time to incorporate new ways of being and seeing the world around them and so on. What I mean here is that those ways which are seen as more desirable are then maintained and held by the upper classes or by those who define themselves as men or as white, meaning that whatever behaviours are seen as socially undesirable are then passed downwards towards the racialised other. The second aspect of this is to recognise that, as the other, we are taught to aspire to those pinnacle focal points of whiteness, of masculinity, of a higher place in the class strata, thereby upholding the supremacy of the racialised system.

Exploring this intersectionally, or through the intersecting lenses of whiteness, patriarchy, and capitalism, it is firstly worth considering the role of capitalism and colonialism. The whole idea of capitalism is built upon the idea of keeping up with the 'Jones', whereby for those of working class, when we see our neighbours get their new car, new television, new whatever it might be, then we feel that we have to keep up with them accordingly (Ham, 2015). The drive to buy the next iPhone or the latest Samsung is a more modern version of this social construction of class built around ideas of capitalism and is especially prevalent in that a good number of people cannot afford to keep maintaining and chasing the latest upgrades in their technology (Böhmke, 2016; Hall, 2011). Because this also fuels inequality, what it also equates to is a level of distress within those who have not. Crime figures for example are often built around ideas that situate themselves around the need for more. So, for example, when we consider the number of phones that have been stolen and the rate of crime within say working class or Black communities, what we have to acknowledge is the socio-economic drive to have more is what in part sits behind some of these statistics.

Another aspect of this, though, when we return to issues of race and racism, is therefore to recognise that race and racism does not exist totally separate from any of the other intersecting oppressions constructed from the systems of supremacy. Racism is not a construct out on its own and will always have ties to homophobia, to sexism, to ableism, to ageism even. The fact that there are a number of persons of colour who find themselves feeling marginalised within the LGBTQ community says a lot about the intersecting interplay between both communities, for example (Various, 2022).

In a similar sort of vein, the ideas behind the split between the second and third waves of feminism, whereby feminists of colour found that their own perspectives and voices were not being heard by their white counterparts, speaks a lot to the intersections of patriarchy and white supremacy (Abd Elaziz, 2021; Collins & Bilge, 2016; hooks, 2016). To even suggest that any one of these systems is more prevalent and more destructive than another misses the point. The mere question alone suggests there is a hierarchy and said question comes from an internalisation of systemic superiority. All three (white supremacy, patriarchy, and capitalism) are in relationship with each other and all three create the systems of oppression that we all endure. In fact, in my view, there is a fourth one, which is based around the idea of religion, but this is a topic that I am not yet ready, or perhaps experienced enough, to explore on my own.

Returning to racism, though, the idea behind exploring race and racism and emphasising and underpinning it by an idea that Sartre brought to bear in his own writings, is multifold. First of all, the unconscious draw to want to own a book which costs me over £50 and yet is no more than 50 pages long, has been with me for a long time. Often that drive to connect to find one's voice is something which sits deep within oneself and which leads to being called forth at some point.

The injunctions against how we might do that, the injunctions against what we might incur when we do so, and the injunctions against whatever feelings are then brought up once we have done so, are all going to be a part of the racist internalisations that silence persons of colour.

Secondly, the fact that an ally such as Sartre, who was himself part of the binary construction of race, felt the need to stand up and say something quite eloquent, meaningful, and powerful about the voice of Blackness, says an awful lot about the permission that I must give myself in relation to this in order to speak up and say my piece. So, whilst I will not necessarily be using poetry as my means of articulating my racial struggle, what I will be using is the creative means and techniques common to psychotherapy and counselling to explore said stress and internalisations. There will be dreams from my own process gathered over the period of time of writing this text, interspersed with some previous stories from my lifetime, thereby designed to highlight the constant, ongoing impact of racial discrimination upon myself.

There will be drawings and perhaps even lyrics to songs selected as another aspect of this route towards racialised recognition presented through my own lens but interpreted and understood as a way of underpinning and showing an understanding again of the unconscious processes provoked through experience of race and racism. The use of the creative here through a sort of more heuristic lens, something which I will talk about later on in this chapter, then also helps oneself to decolonise the ways in which we might understand racism.

The essential part to this decolonisation of understanding of racism, is that we often look at racism through a very quantitative lens. Somebody has an experience of being marginalised, maybe they have to prove it at work; for example, they have to go away and prove it in a Court of Law, then on the balance of probabilities there is a suggestion that this thing happened or it did not happen, and a person on the receiving end may or may not see a payout or satisfaction through the legal systems of our countries, through studies of microaggressions, or the experiences of marginalisation in mental health services (Besley, 2021; Cobb et al., 2020; Rockett et al., 2006; Sue et al., 2007). Yet, when we talk about racism, what often gets missed, hence the creative means that I may well be employing today, is the unspoken, internalised, unconscious whispers of hatred that we endure when we encounter, or when we are, the racialised other.

This book will therefore take a vastly different approach to texts like Diangelo's *White Fragility*, whereby the idea of the fragility of whiteness when encountering Blackness, whilst well-made and well expressed, fails to recognise that it is embedded within the binary nature of racial construction (Diangelo, 2018). I have in previous texts written about the threat to one's own egoic structure for whiteness when encountering Blackness and also the struggle against the internalised and silencing mechanisms which persons of Blackness hold when encountering whiteness and having to find their voice. Here though, this book will also consider the system of whiteness which influences all of us and hinders the racial identities of those who identify as white as well as those who are the other.

Within this vastly different and collectively relational exploration, what will be explored is how the central pillars of white supremacy – capitalism and colonialism and patriarchy – have been created in conjunction with centralising themselves in the construction of systemic whiteness. This is a whiteness, though, by which we are all identified. So be it; because we are Jewish, Romany, Māori, South Asian, Black African or another identity, a part of our racialised identity will have been constructed as the shadow mirror of whiteness.

Therefore, in writing this book about racism and exploring this immense and important topic, one of the things to recognise is that this is not just a book for persons of colour. There will be questions to be answered by all of us as we go through this text in how we explore our racial identity, and much of what I will be discussing and laying out before yourselves can be utilised by anyone from any of the racial categorisations in their own exploration of what it is to be racialised, either as a subject or other, as well.

Methodological underpinnings

Given that race is therefore a collective relational construct, it makes no sense to then just select ways of working and understanding race that do not employ a more relational perspective as well. This is a colonised way of making sense and meaning of the world around us, whereby, to borrow from an idea posited by Sontag (2009), we attempt to reach a point of domination through the analysis of our topic area. What this also does is take us away from what we do as counsellors and psychotherapists, which is look at a phenomenon through the lens of the relationship between client and therapist. Within the context of this book, it therefore makes sense that if we are going to explore issues of race, then we need to be using more relational means to broaden out and explore this topic.

Phenomenology has been selected as the way in which I am going to do this in this instance. The reasons for this are multifold. First, experiences of racism are not, as I have previously said, just cognitive. They are not just something which you experience and think about and wander away from. In fact, in many instances, when we endure experiences of racism, the victim goes away, overthinks the issues; the experience bothers said person for days or more onwards.

The relational aspect of this is therefore important. What was the experience that I went through when I encountered the subject? What messages do I give myself to make it OK for the subject to make their statement, their joke, their slur towards me? How do they contrast to how I truly feel about being racially assessed, objectified, or abused? Questions like this when we start to work with issues of race and racism then allow us to start thinking and feeling about just what has occurred and what we might be splitting ourselves into.

The idea of splitting is hugely important to this book. A term coined by psychodynamic psychotherapists, splitting involves the ridding oneself of different memories, feelings and experiences, which are often then forced into the unconscious (Jacobs, 2003; Sletvold, 2013). This is all also done in service to the ego in early developmental years (Bowlby, 1973). When we consider the issue of splitting with regard to racism, though, there is another crucial factor here. When we over-think these experiences, what often happens is we have split ourselves between our mind and our body. Whereas the mind has been taught by persons who identify as the racialised others to put their experience to one side, what often happens is the body, in its trauma response to an experience of racial abuse, gets stuck with trying to work out what has happened and pushes this issue back to the forefront of their physical and mental self. Neurologically this is no different to how trauma gets stuck in the neural pathways of the brain and this triangulation of approaches through the body and the brain suggests that actually racism is a form of trauma and that for persons as the racialised other these experiences of trauma are almost daily occurrences (Sletvold, 2013; van der Kolk, 2015).

So, when we have experiences of racism, the relationship between us and the other person and that incident is also mirrored by the relationship between our-selves and the mind/body split. There is a triangulation that goes on in all these instances. This is the first part to recognise. The second part is that a phenomeno-logical exploration of racism then becomes the perfect vehicle by which we can work with the experiential experiences of a traumatic incident like racism, utilising the body-work ideas of philosophers such as Merleau-Ponty who recognised that phenomenology is a physical experience, not just a theoretical and therefore airy or heady one (Merleau-ponty, 1962, 2002).

To expand a bit further, the branch of phenomenology that I am utilising here moves us beyond aeolian logic and takes us further towards a different type of knowing and understanding and one that is no less important from a scientific standpoint (Cox & Thielgaard, 1986). Recognising that experiences of racism im-pact upon ourselves on a physiological level then opens the door to what that physi-ological level might be, how these experiences might be experienced and how we can better understand and recognise just what racism is. If we were going towards a more scientific perspective, we could look at the work of Tull and others (Butler et al., 2002; Tull et al., 1999) and their work out of the University of the Carib-bean, who recognise that experiences of marginalisation and racism were at least partly responsible for the increased levels of obesity and diabetes in Caribbean populations.

Other angles psychologists have looked at include the experiences of refugees to the United Kingdom, some of which will have been based around experiences of racism, and how this has led to higher levels of alcohol abuse, self-harm, and suicidal ideation within those communities (Bhui et al., 2007). When paired against other forms of marginalisation, prejudice and homophobia, then what we start to also get is another form of triangulation is the recognition that the hate that is meted out against minorities and this will include racialised minorities, leads to different or higher levels of depression and suicidality (Feinstein et al., 2012; Lick et al., 2013).

These early explorations of racism from a more scientific standpoint then lay out a benchmark upon which this more phenomenological exploration can build. This

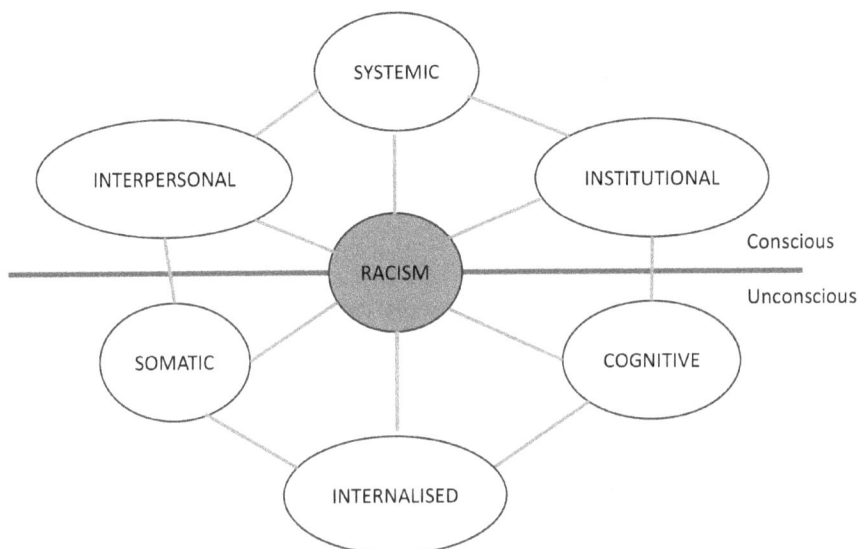

Figure 1.1 Conscious and unconscious racism

is important, given that without it we are left floundering in a sea of unknowing as to just what racism actually is.

The next idea to factor in here if we are going to look at ideas of what racism is, is held in Figure 1.1. Figure 1.1 maps out the types of racism which we will be exploring in this volume. What we see here is *systemic racism, institutional racism, unconscious racism,* and *interpersonal racism* – all floating around a central point. No one of these different forms or experiences of racism is any more or less important than the other, but often what happens in explorations of race and racism is that we focus in on perhaps one or two of these areas, leaving out the others.

For example, *institutional racism* is prevalent in many different environments. Particular examples are often seen in organisations which, in their diversity hires, either tokenise their approach to equality, diversity, and inclusion by just bringing in somebody of colour, or of difference, who may have a certain position and a role but no power to create change (Flores Niemann, 1999). Or, alternatively, there is no difference or diversity held within the organisation because, whilst there are those organisations who do not believe in culture wars, any sort of movement towards a more inclusive environment is one that has to be suppressed and excluded. The example below speaks to this experience of institutional racism:

> I remember once, in particular, an experience of a transpersonal organisation who had asked me to come and speak to them about EDI, so therefore I was invited in as a speaker. Yet, in the days in the run up to this presentation the amount of vilification and anger at my even being present to speak at their conference

meant that actually doing so became a slightly more fraught affair than it needed to be. Whilst presenting at said organisation, one of the participants who was in a position of power within said organisation, called out my work for dividing groups and not making them more inclusive. This sort of ran counter to the information that I had been given by the organisers, who had said that their organisation was exclusive and was not as inclusive as it could have been.

Racism in this organisation's instance, in its institutional sense, actually involved the splitting and distancing themselves of responsibility for their own exclusivity, projecting this onto an invited speaker who was there to actually explore said experiences with them. The irony of that experience was that in the years following, notification was received by myself which stated that in fact nothing much had changed within the organisation; it was still as white and as old and as fixed in its opinions as it was previously. *Institutional racism* in this instance is something whereby the institute, the organisation, works within itself to maintain its structures of superiority, separateness, eliteness, based around a patriarchal, white supremacist idea.

The next one to consider is obvious – it has to be *systemic racism*. The racism which is built into a system in ways that are incredibly subtle but are far reaching and therefore quite horrific in some instances. One of the strangest and yet most destructive and hateful examples involves the fact that Black women in the United Kingdom are four times more likely to die in childbirth than white women (Draper et al., 2022). In exploring this and working with a colleague around the level of attention paid to the physiology of women of colour, be they Black, Asian, Indian, or other, alongside white women within maternity trainings, what I was often told was that everything they were taught was from a very white perspective. There was no consideration of the diverse levels of pain, resilience, or whatever else that women of difference are able to endure. There was also no recognition of the layers of racism that have gone on beforehand for women of difference and of colour in the establishing of the scientific principles of the Global North.

One of the earliest examples of this was the treatment meted out on Black women by the scientific community in the research and implementation of anaesthesia in operations, whereby a number of women of colour would have been operated upon without any anaesthetic to ascertain their pain threshold and the level and dosage therefore which would have been required for white women (Saini, 2019). The fact that race and racism has also been used in many other ways, against many other groups within the scientific world suggests that there is a systemic problem that sits within the medical community. This is no different to the world of mental health, whereby ideas of what it is and what it is not to be human, healthy, and mentally 'sane' have often led to the marginalisation and the over-medicalisation of persons of colour and of racial difference (Barnham, 2023).

Perhaps the most obvious within this category has to come from the police forces, not just of the United Kingdom but of America, France, and other countries in the Global North. The over-preponderance of persons of colour who are either incarcerated, murdered, stop and searched, harassed, or unfairly and unjustly charged for crimes is such a massive statistic that to suggest that racism does not exist and is not a part of these experiences is to project a systemic blindness at the level of the problem (Various, 2021a).

The systemic harassment of many separate groups based upon their racial difference, the political vilification of said groups as well, based upon the fact that they are migrants, or the fact that they are from former colonies, is a common experience of persons of racial difference coming to the Global North. To keep suggesting that these things do not matter, that things have not happened, that these things do not occur, is to actually whitewash the memories and experiences of those people for whom this is a daily occurrence.

From the experience of this seven-year-old boy who, whilst in a store was told he needed to 'watch his tone' and that, 'you people are always getting into trouble', to the experiences of this over 50-year-old man who, in a discussion around the reasons why he would be leaving an organisation based upon the racism held within it, was told to 'watch his tone'. The nearly 50 years in between showed that man that these experiences were not only exactly the same but that racism in these situations was about power over the other.

Interpersonal racism is an aspect which we probably experience most of all but are often least aware of. It is that incident at the very beginning of this chapter; it is those instances which I will detail at the beginning of each chapter that have happened to myself; it is the moments for every person reading this book, be they Jewish, of colour, Indian, Asian, when they have been put down, objectified, stereotyped, thingified, in an experience and interaction with somebody else who they previously thought they could trust, perhaps, or who they met only for an instance, never to see again. To paraphrase something expressed by the comedian Chris Rock, you always have to be on the lookout for racism because you can never be quite sure when it is going to occur, whilst knowing full well that at some point today, tomorrow, next week, next month, it will occur. It will happen (Callner, 2008).

The next one here is why this book, written by a psychotherapist, is especially important. The internalisation of racist moments and racism experiences, or *internalised racism*, actually leaves a scar which sits deep within the psyche. So therefore, any exploration around what racism is has to take into account these four areas, and in particular has to look at the internalised racist that leads us to want to change our colour; that leads us to want to code switch; that leads us to want to perform, to hide, to silence ourselves; that fears speaking up, less we be labelled or denigrated or destroyed in some way; or some other means of internalisation which I have not yet mentioned or discussed.

Where this book is particularly poignant is in the inclusion of both *somatic racism* and *cognitive racism*. In the explorations and research for this book, recognising that there is a layer before we come to the *internalised racism* layer is important. For something to sit deep within us, within our unconscious, there has to be both a mental and embodied disconnect from the truth, from the reality of our experience when we endure racism. This therefore brings racism into the realm of both trauma and emotional abuse.

Figure 1.1 and the breadth and range of racist experiences then starts to give us that phenomenological framework around racism which this book is most concerned with.

Collective experiences of racism

bell hooks (2016) wrote that patriarchy is not about gender, and in texts where I have previously written about race, I recognise that racism and race are not about colour. The laziness in these previous assumptions will always make any argument about racism an 'Us' and 'Them' binary, an argument structure very much rooted within the philosophical paradigms of the Global North.

To understand racism, and to bring it more into line with the phenomenological approach utilised in this text, Figure 1.2 is important. Firstly, Systemic Whiteness, which sits at the centre of Figure 1.2, has nothing to do with white colour. Where it was constructed from in its earliest form, was the idea that if one was upper class and white and English, or of a similar standing within a European country, then one held power and sway over the other (Turner, 2023). In these instances, the other would be the working classes and those from the Celtic nations. Whiteness has evolved over a period to incorporate other groups and it is important to recognise that many of those incorporations, be they individual or collective, will not be white in colour.

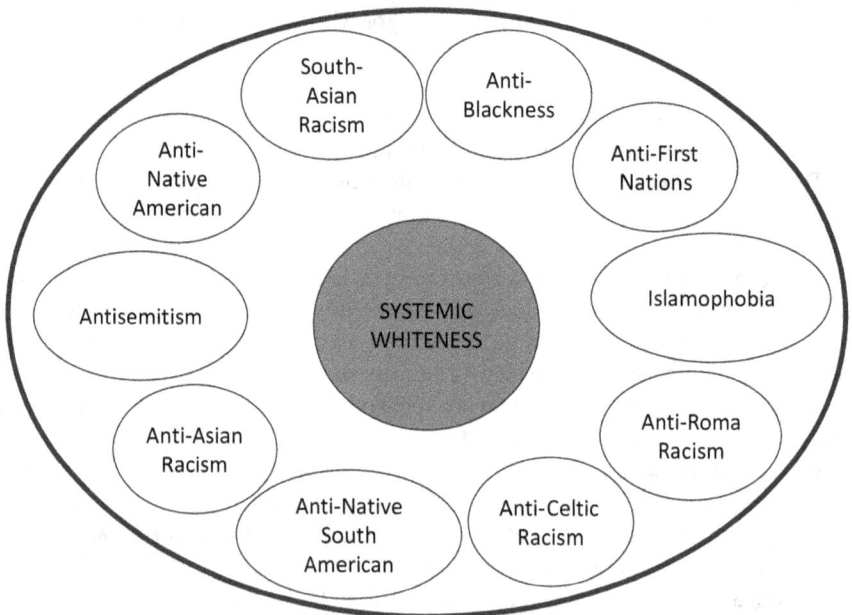

Figure 1.2 Forms of racism

In the autumn of 2022 in the United Kingdom, the far-right government of the Conservatives then elected within themselves a non-white prime minister to uphold their many far-right ideals. The fact that this man was of wealth and standing is in many ways just as important as the fact of his colour. This is conversely relevant to note because when we look at some of the ways and experiences of racism which sit around that centralised block within Figure 1.2, what we see is even on that most basic level that many of the groups that we are talking about are not Black. The *Roma* peoples who have a huge and rich history in and around Europe, are in many ways not seen as Black but they are not white either and the prejudice and hatred meted out against them means that they are often marginalised, more so than many other groups (Ciaian & Kancs, 2019; Lagos et al., 2022).

A more obvious example, if one likes, comes in the form of *antisemitism*, which in its own way is another form of racism. It is important here to recognise the obviousness of this through the marginalisation and the hatred forced upon Jewish peoples for a couple of millennia, culminating in the atrocities of the Second World War and the formation of Israel (Judaken, 1999; Quispel, 1999). So already we see that racism is not about colour. It is about an experience of hatred based around the idea that one is seen as less than ideal, less than systemically white. Racism has its roots in supremacy, not just the supremacy of whiteness but the supremacy of patriarchy and, more importantly perhaps, capitalism.

Other areas earmarked within Figure 1.2 include the obvious sort of anti-Blackness which I personally would have experienced at varying points in my life and career. I say life, because I walk through a white European world and I say career because, even as a counsellor and psychotherapist, these experiences of anti-Blackness, of professionals and students choosing to whitesplain my job back to me, are forms of racism that one often struggles to challenge. We will look further at some of these ideas and experiences in other parts of this book.

Anti-South Asian rhetoric is another form of racism which comes out from the centre and the marginalisation of certain groups after the end of colonialism – groups who came to the Global North because they were told that this was their home as well, only to be met by levels of hatred and anger and marginalisation – meant that it has taken at least a good couple of generations for persons of South Asian descent to find a place of acceptance (Mui & Kang, 2006).

One of the more recently prolific for varying international reasons is the level of *Islamophobia* which sits in and around our cultures, especially post-911. This is a form of hatred that is often stoked politically, whereby whole groups are marked out as abusers to be hated and vilified, thereby giving credence to the cries of the far right and institutes such as the English Defence League as they march the streets searching for persons of Islamic descent to assault and abuse (Stone, 2016). Issues of racism, though, have been exported across the world and ideas of anti-Blackness, Islamophobia, anti-Asian rhetoric also sit in and around the world within colonised countries across the board.

Another example, the recent racist silencing of the *First Nation*'s Initiative to provide them with a voice in Australia was very much racist rhetoric and the manipulation of whole groups of people (Manathunga et al., 2020), given that these were a people who have endured the ravages of systemic racism, and white supremacy will have been doubly painful for a whole swathe of peoples (McLane et al., 2022; Stelkia, 2023). *Native Americans* in the United States and North America have often suffered at the hand of racist ideas, so much so that their annihilation across part of a whole continent is still one of the greatest national tragedies to befall a set people (Dudley, 2017). This is something which is also echoed to the north in Canada and in particular I draw a comparison between the treatment of children in Canada and the treatment and marginalisation of children in Australia, whereby their removal from their families with the idea being to civilise said populations was driven by the racist idea that actually they were less than human and needed to be brought under some form of systemic control (Stelkia, 2023).

One of the last areas I would like to consider in Figure 1.2 is therefore the *Indigenous South Americans* whose descendants, alongside those of darker colours, make up the preponderance of the favelas in Brazil, for example, and who have suffered even more than those of a more European descent and shading within South America (Benicio & Craveiro, n.d.; Maranhão & Knijnik, 2011).

This brief list here is not exclusive and it has of course left out a sizeable number of groupings and ideas about what systemic whiteness has actually engendered in the forms of racism. The anti-Blackness or anti-otherness of other cultures across the globe, such as within say China, is an area which I cannot consider in this book. Yet what this more relational perspective on the centralised positioning of whiteness does, is it recognises that racism and the hatred of the other, based upon social constructed ideals of race, is a phenomenon which circles all of us in some way. This is the importance of a book like this, that it does not just focus on one strand of anti-Blackness and it takes a more phenomenological and therefore expansive vision point when trying to consider and explore areas where this might occur.

Summary

This chapter therefore outlines the different layers which I believe intersect in experiences of racism. At no point is racism just a singular experience. There is always a relational one and what this means is the relationship between ourselves and our family, our culture, our background, the society we are raised within, the institutions we inhabit and so on, but it is also a relationship which becomes internalised and becomes one within ourselves. The importance of these facets is designed in concert to show how they actually impact upon us on a deeper psychological level which can only be explored through using creativity and/or dream work.

This book is not designed to see these experiences as hopeless, as hope is always there. Chapter 5, 'The Privilege of Vulnerability versus the Invincibility of Suffering', presents us with a route through the malaise of racism. For many generations, individuals, groups, peoples, have used their suffering as a benchmark from which they have developed voices to present poetry, art, song, and other forms of creativity to the wider masses. The exploration of these experiences, which would have otherwise left them devoid of hope or meaning, has often been a route through enduring the deeper-seated layers of racism and oppression most of us have encountered.

To start our journey, though, in exploring just what racism is from within psychotherapeutic and phenomenological frameworks, it is best for us to venture outside and explore some of the areas in which racism occurs, the forms that it inhabits, and the ways in which it impacts upon many of us, whilst also offering a more psychological lens within which to view these experiences. This is the reason this next chapter is called 'The Phenomenology of Racism'.

References

Abd Elaziz, H. G. (2021). Against white feminism: Notes on disruption, by Rafia Zakaria. W. W. Norton, 2021. *Women's Studies*, *51*(2), 268–270. https://doi.org/10.1080/00497878. 2021.2014837

Aosved, A. C., Long, P. J., & Voller, E. K. (2009). Measuring sexism, racism, sexual prejudice, ageism, classism, and religious intolerance: The intolerant Schema Measure. *Journal of Applied Social Psychology*, *39*(10), 2321–2354. https://doi.org/10.1111/j.1559-1816.2009.00528.x

Barnes, E. (2016). *The Minority Body: a theory of disability*. Oxford University Press.

Barnham, P. (2023). *Outrageous reason: Madness and race in Britain and Empire*. PCCS Books.

Beauvoir, S. de. (2010). *The Second Sex*. Alfred A. Knopf.

Benicio, J. C., & Craveiro, S. (n.d.). *Prejudice, Diversity, Human Rights and Diversity-valuing Policy: a Critical Analysis of Governmental Initiatives to Promote Diversity in the Workforce in Brazil*. 1–22.

Besley, J. (2021). Euro 2020: FA condemns racist abuse of England players after shootout defeat. *Independent Online*. www.independent.co.uk/sport/football/saka-sancho-rashford-racism-england-euros-b1882325.html

Bhui, K., McKenzie, K., & Rasul, F. (2007). Rates, risk factors & methods of self harm among minority ethnic groups in the UK: A systematic review. *BMC Public Health*, *7*. https://doi.org/10.1186/1471-2458-7-336

Böhmke, W. (2016). Reflecting on social psychology and global neo-liberal capitalism. *Psychology in Society*, *52*, 101–102. https://doi.org/10.17159/2309-8708/2016/n52a14

Bowlby, J. (1973). *Separation*. Pimlico.

Butler, C., Tull, E. S., Chambers, E. C., Taylor, J., & Ph, D. (2002). Internalised racism, body fat distribution, and abnormal fasting glucose among Caribbean women in Dominica, West Indies. *Journal of the National Medical Association*, *94*(3), 143–148.

Callner, M. (2008). *Chris Rock: Kill the Messenger* (p. 1). HBO. www.imdb.com/title/tt1213574/

Ciaian, P., & Kancs, D. (2019). Marginalisation of Roma: Root causes and possible policy actions. *European Review*, *27*(1), 115–130. https://doi.org/10.1017/S106279871800056X

Clement, J. (2014). *Widow Basquiat*. Canongate Books.

Cobb, S., Javanbakht, A., Soltani, E. K., Bazargan, M., & Assari, S. (2020). Racial difference in the relationship between health and happiness in the United States. *Psychology Research and Behavior Management*, *13*. https://doi.org/10.2147/PRBM.S248633

Collins, P. H., & Bilge, S. (2016). *Intersectionality: Key concepts*. Polity Press.

Cooke, S. (2016). *A Change Gonna Come*. Portrait of a Legend (1951–1964). https://www.youtube.com/watch?v=wEBlaMOmKV4

Cox, M., & Thielgaard, A. (1986). *Mutative metaphors in psychotherapy: The Aeolian mode*. Tavistock.

Diangelo, R. (2018). *White fragility: Why it's so hard for white people to talk about racism*. Beacon Press.

Draper, E. S., Gallimore, I. D., Smith, L. K., Matthews, R. J., Fenton, A. C., Kurinczuk, J. J., Smith, P. W., & Manktelow, B. N. (2022). *MBRRACE-UK Perinatal Mortality Surveillance Report, UK Perinatal Deaths for Births from January to December 2020* (Issue 2020).

Du Bois, W. E. (1903). *The souls of Black folk*. Amazon Classics.

Dudley, M. Q. (2017). A library matter of genocide: The Library of Congress and the historiography of the Native American Holocaust. *International Indigenous Policy Journal, 8*(2). https://doi.org/10.18584/iipj.2017.8.2.9

Ellis, E. (2021). *The race conversation: An essential guide to creating life-changing dialogue*. Confer Books.

Eminem. (2017). *Untouchable*. Revival. https://www.youtube.com/watch?v=56KYMMGudcU

Feinstein, B., Goldfried, M. R., & Davila, J. (2012). The relationship between experiences of discrimination and mental health among lesbians and gay men: An examination of internalized homonegativity and rejection sensitivity as potential mechanisms. *Journal of Consulting and Clinical Psychology, 80*(5), 917–927. https://doi.org/10.1037/a0029425

Flores Niemann, Y. (1999). The making of a token: A case study of stereotype threat, stigma, racism, and tokenism in academe. *Frontiers: A Journal of Women Studies, 20*(1), 111–134.

Gilligan, C. (1995). Hearing the difference, theorising connection. *Bloomington, 10*(2), 120–122.

Hall, S. (2011). The neo-liberal revolution. *Cultural Studies, 25*(6), 705–728. https://doi.org/10.1080/09502386.2011.619886

Ham, B.-C. (2015). *The burnout society*. Stamford University Press.

hooks, B. (2016). Feminism is for everybody. In *Ideals and Ideologies: A Reader*. https://doi.org/10.4324/9781315625546

Jacobs, M. (2003). *Sigmund Freud: Key figures in counselling and psychotherapy* (2nd ed.). Sage.

Judaken, J. (1999). The queer Jew: Gender, sexuality and Jean-Paul Sartre's anti-antisemitism. *Patterns of Prejudice, 33*(3), 45–63. https://doi.org/10.1080/003132299128810623

Julaud, J.-J. (2019). *Anthologie des la Nuvelle Poesie Negre et Malgache de langue Française*. First.

Kinouani, G. (2021). *Living while Black: The essential guide to overcoming racial trauma*. Ebury Press.

Lagos, T. G., Singh, Y., Pace, A., Stone, E., Wu, H., Yan, H., & Forbes-Luong, S. (2022). Studying abroad meets marginalization: Roma of Greece, autoethnography, and academic tourism. *Journal of Tourism Management Research, 9*(2), 125–139. https://doi.org/10.18488/31.v9i2.3138

Lick, D. J., Durso, L. E., & Johnson, K. L. (2013). Minority stress and physical health among sexual minorities. *Perspectives on Psychological Science, 8*(5), 521–548. https://doi.org/10.1177/1745691613497965

Manathunga, C., Davidow, S., Williams, P., Gilbey, K., Bunda, T., Raciti, M., & Stanton, S. (2020). Decolonisation through poetry: Building first nations' voice and promoting truth-telling. *Education as Change, 24*, 1–24. https://doi.org/10.25159/1947-9417/7765

Maranhão, T. F., & Knijnik, J. (2011). Futebol mulato : Racial constructs in Brazilian football. *Cosmopolitan Civil Societies Journal, 3*(2), 55–71.

McLane, P., Mackey, L., Holroyd, B. R., Fitzpatrick, K., Healy, C., Rittenbach, K., Plume, T. B., Bill, L., Bird, A., Healy, B., Janvier, K., Louis, E., & Barnabe, C. (2022). Impacts of racism on First Nations patients' emergency care: Results of a thematic analysis of healthcare provider interviews in Alberta, Canada. *BMC Health Services Research, 22*(1), 1–18. https://doi.org/10.1186/s12913-022-08129-5

Merleau-ponty, M. (1962). *The phenomenology of perception*. Routledge.

Merleau-ponty, M. (2002). *The world of perception*. Routledge.

Mui, A. C., & Kang, S. Y. (2006). Acculturation stress and depression among Asian immigrant elders. *Social Work, 51*(3), 243–255. https://doi.org/10.1093/sw/51.3.243

Quispel, C. (1999). Faithful servants and dangerous beasts: Race, nationalism and historical mythmaking. *Patterns of Prejudice, 33*(3). https://doi.org/10.1080/003132299128810614

Rockett, I. R. H., Samora, J. B., & Coben, J. H. (2006). The black–white suicide paradox: Possible effects of misclassification. *Social Science and Medicine, 63*(8), 2165–2175. https://doi.org/10.1016/j.socscimed.2006.05.017

Saini, A. (2019). *Superior: The return of race science*. Harper Collins.

Sartre, J. (1948). *Black Orpheus*. Presence Africaine.

Sletvold, J. (2013). The ego and the id revisited: Freud and Damasio on the body ego/self. *The International Journal of Psycho-Analysis, 94*(5), 1019–1032. https://doi.org/10.1111/1745-8315.12097

Sontag, S. (2009). *Against interpretation and other essays*. Penguin Classics.

Stelkia, K. (2023). Structural racism as an ecosystem: An exploratory study on how structural racism influences chronic disease and health and wellbeing of First Nations in Canada. *International Journal of Environmental Research and Public Health, 20*(10). https://doi.org/10.3390/ijerph20105851

Stone, J. (2016). EU Referendum: Baroness Warsi subjected to Islamophobic abuse by Brexit supporters after defecting. *Independent Online*. www.independent.co.uk/news/uk/politics/eu-referendum-baroness-warsi-defect-islamophobic-abuse-brexit-supporters-remain-leave-a7091076.html

Sue, D. W., Capodilupo, C. M., Torino, G. C., Bucceri, J. M., Holder, A. M. B., Nadal, K. L., & Esquilin, M. (2007). Racial microaggressions in everyday life: Implications for clinical practice. *American Psychologist, 62*(4), 271–286. https://doi.org/10.1037/0003-066X.62.4.271

Tull, S. E., Wickramasuriya, T., Taylor, J., Smith-Burns, V., Brown, M., Champagnie, G., Daye, K., Donaldson, K., Solomon, N., Walker, S., Fraser, H., & Jordan, O. W. (1999). Relationship of internalized racism to abdominal obesity and blood pressure in Afro-Caribbean women. *Journal of the National Medical Association, 91*(8), 447–452. www.pubmedcentral.nih.gov/articlerender.fcgi?artid=2608441&tool=pmcentrez&rendertype=abstract

Turner, D. D. L. (2018). You shall not replace us!: White Supremacy, psychotherapy and decolonisation. *Journal of Critical Psychology Counselling and Psychotherapy, 18*(1), 1–12.

Turner, D. D. L. (2023). *The psychology of supremacy*. Routledge.

van der Kolk, B. (2015). *The body keeps the score: Mind, brain and body in the transformation of trauma* (1st ed.). Penguin Books.

Various. (2019). *Summary: The social construction of difference*. Tagtow. https://blogs.oregonstate.edu/tagtow/2019/10/04/summary-the-social-construction-of-difference/

Various. (2020). *George Floyd Death*. BBC News. www.bbc.co.uk/news/topics/cv7wlylxzg1t/george-floyd-death

Various. (2021a). *Ethnicity Facts and Figures: Stop and Search Statistics*. GOV.UK. www.ethnicity-facts-figures.service.gov.uk/crime-justice-and-the-law/policing/stop-and-search/latest#by-ethnicity

Various. (2021b). *Has George Floyd Changed Britain?* ITV. www.itv.com/presscentre/ep1week19/trevor-mcdonald-charlene-white-has-george-floyd-changed-britain#

Various. (2022). *Queering Psychotherapy* (J. C. Czyzselska (ed.)). Karnac Books.

Chapter 2

The Phenomenology of Racism

Introduction

To underline the points made in this chapter, I am opening with an example of racism from my own family history rooted in Empire and colonialism:

Example:

My mother arrived in the United Kingdom as part of the Windrush generation in the late 1950s. She travelled from Trinidad to the United Kingdom to train as a nurse because this is what she always wanted to do with her life. She met my father in a London hospital whilst he was working as an ambulance driver. They courted and over a period, they got closer and decided to get married. My father, though, arrived in the UK towards the end of the Second World War. He fought in the D-Day Landings and played an active role in the Royal Air Force in the struggle against Nazism and the attempts to end the war.

Both my parents struggled in their times in the United Kingdom. Both were raised during a period of colonialism where they believed themselves to be very much British. They had been taught the English language, educated within an English curriculum, and sought out the chance to come to the United Kingdom as a way of not just getting away from their homelands in the Caribbean but also to establish themselves in an England born out of the fantasy ideals they had been taught and that they had bought into. In varying ways, both their arrivals were met with levels of racism and hatred.

My father found himself very much marginalised whilst a member of the Commonwealth forces in the United Kingdom. He struggled to find both friends and people to relate to outside of his own community made up of other men and occasional women in the forces who were also raised in the colonies. My mother's experience was similar and at the same time different and more insidious. Her arrival in the United Kingdom was at a time when there were numerous objections, political and otherwise, to persons of

DOI: 10.4324/9781003508854-2

difference coming to the United Kingdom. When she arrived, she was met with signs outside boarding houses and lodges which read 'No Blacks, No Irish and No dogs', to the extent that these experiences, and many others in hospitals, where she was often told by patients they did not want to work with 'a blackee, a nig nog', or even worse, meant that she had to endure a level of hatred she had not believed that she would encounter when she first ventured out from Trinidad.

Both of my parents' experiences were not just interpersonal ones. Often these were underpinned by the politics of their day. My father arriving at the end of the War coincided with the rise of the far right in the East End of London where Mosley and his Black Shirts were marching the streets of London campaigning against the rise of immigration from the former colonies. He arrived in a place riddled with racism and, although he survived and made his way through, there were struggles, both cultural and political, which had huge impacts upon how he related to others around him and his own family.

My mother found a different path. In my experience of her, she made herself ever more ingratiating in her smiling, performative nature, trying as hard as she could to fit in, to comply, to be a part of English culture. So, whilst she would still prepare Caribbean foods, when we were out and socialising, or when the local vicar came to visit, the norms of her Trinidadian and West Indian culture were often left on the back burner in order for her to present herself as acceptable and English.

In a television interview on Sunday the 9th of September 2024, the British Prime Minister, Sir Keir Starmer, stated that he did not believe that racism existed in this country. His comment, following on from a discussion about the far-right leanings of origins of the recent race riots across the country, led to many persons of racial difference rolling their eyes in disdain. This was a refrain posted again and again by English politicians, this idea that racism does not exist.

My parents' example, just one of many presented in this book, show just how nonsensical Starmer's views were. Given that race is a social construct built out of the supremacy of whiteness, to say that racism does not exist does not so much deny the primacy that whiteness holds, but reinforces white supremacy and its ability to negate the presence of the racialised other. The experiences of those who were abused, spat upon, beaten up, or otherwise threatened – experiences meted out upon them because of their colour or racial differences – happened because there was a sense of whiteness feeling threatened.

The other aspect this chapter highlights is that race is a core construct of the cultural fabric of the Global North. This is one of the reasons why it is tough, although I will not say impossible, to disrupt and stop racism; a whole cultural system is built out of the socially constructed fabric of racial superiority. To end racism, therefore, means that a whole culture has to question its identity in relation to race, be it on all sides of this phenomenological construction. This is the importance of a book like this, in that it gets to the root of just what race is, and how it binds so many to its self-perpetuating existential core.

Phenomenology fits this bill well and this is the reason this book is entitled *A Phenomenology of Racism in Counselling and Psychotherapy*. Phenomenological explorations are, by their very nature, relational. They are relational with regard to the interpersonal, but they are also relational with regard to how we interact with ourselves. For example, the relationship between the ego, the id, and the super-ego, or the false self and the shadow (Jacobs, 2003). This chapter will therefore initially look to establish a phenomenological framework for this work before then exploring how racism, as an experience, as a relational experience, then impacts upon us all as the racialised other in more ways than we could ever possibly have understood.

Phenomenology and embodied racism

Phenomenology in its inception is an idea created by Husserl, the philosopher who, in the 1900s, recognised that how we make sense of our world is very different to perhaps some of the more scientific ways that were being established in exactly that same period (Husserl, 2012; Moerer-Urdahl & Creswell, 2004). This movement away from the more aeolian, or cognitive, methods of understanding our world thereby gave space for a more relational way of understanding how we interact with the world and how we make sense of our experiences (Cox & Thielgaard, 1986).

This more relational way of understanding the environment that we live within, and our experiences within it, is something which was built upon by numerous thinkers and philosophers within that phenomenological tradition. From the likes of Heidegger, to Hegel, to Levinas, numerous theorists since phenomenology's inception have built upon the ideas of Husserl and taken phenomenology along a number of interesting and intuitive routes (Hegel, 1976; Heidegger, 2010; Levinas, 1961).

For my own work though, it is the work of Merleau-Ponty (1962, 2002) who forms the bedrock of my study and this book. The reason for his inclusion is that Merleau-Ponty's ideas incorporated the work of the body and, given that racism is not just something which happens to us outside of ourselves, it is important to understand not just the cognitive but also the embodied experience of racism that we all encounter. Merleau-Ponty's work, much like phenomenology also takes us in the direction towards a more post-humanistic way of understanding this phenomenon of racism.

What I mean by post-humanism is that there are a number of philosophers who recognise that one of the end goals of humanistic philosophy is that it moves itself away from the hierarchy embedded within the cultural structures of the Global North, returning it to a more relational experience embedded within and alongside the world around and inside of ourselves (Fernando, 2020; Kamwangamalu, 1999; Keeling & Lehman, 2018). The body is a route towards that, or more importantly, the breaking of the established hierarchy of mind over body that psychodynamic theorists, for example Lacan, have contemplated for a number of years (Homer, 2007).

In any process of individuation, as posited by Carl Jung (Stein, 2005), where we divest ourselves from the cultural and internalised structures which bind and make us conform, there is a return to the interdependent relationship between self and others (with other being internal and external). In this continued process of post-humanistic growth, there is also a returning of the re-igniting of the humanity of the other within our own eyes, or under our own gaze (Jung, 1959). This phenomenological approach when we understand racism and its multiple experiences is, in my view, one of the drivers behind the sheer number of books and texts from persons of colour who have written about their own racial experiences over the past ten years (Andrews, 2016; Andrews & Palmer, 2013; Ellis, 2021; Kinouani, 2021).

In building these narratives and telling these stories of racist experiences, both personal and on counselling and psychology training courses, what we are also starting to see is a recognition and a re-alignment of some institutions and in some ways also some individuals, who have recognised their own complicity in the racist oppression of their own peers. This is not to blame those organisations or those persons, but it is to remind them that they are as much co-opted by these intersections of capitalism, white supremacy, and patriarchy which form the cultural super-egoic framework for racism as any of us are. And that any efforts to work through the need to be seen and heard as raised within *Example 2*, involves the returning of the voice of the other, with the other having a safe enough space to be seen, heard, witnessed, and empathised with.

Returning to the conjunction of phenomenology and the silencing of the racialised other in any discourse around racism adds to the often unexpressed and overarching need for certain groups and individuals to deny racism's presence in the world (Neville et al., 2013). Hatred though is a human condition, without it there can be no love. Racism is a human construction, and without it there can be no hierarchy of race. However, when the racialised other enables themselves and re-discovers their voice to speak up about their experience of racism, the hatred meted out against the racialised other, whilst initially leading to conflict, must inevitably lead to a realignment of purposes and principles which must bring change.

When I say change though, I do not necessarily mean that sort of more idealistic, happily ever after idea of change; what I mean here is that change involves a moving forward in the understanding of the other and oneself. A growth as human beings, a movement beyond the racialised shackles which bind both subject and other in a co-dependent relationship and dance of mirror identities.

However, in order for us to understand just how wide ranging this phenomenological exploration and experience of racism actually is, it is important that we actually lay the groundwork for those externalised experiences of racism which may sit around us but the range of which we may not really be aware of. The purpose of the next stage of this chapter is to map out the phenomenology of racism, as much as it is possible for one person to do. This is not to say that my list presented further on in this text is exhaustive. It is, though, to start a wider debate about just how far-reaching racism is under the intersections of white supremacy, capitalism, and patriarchy.

Intersections of race

I want to start this section with a clear statement. Race is a construct where originally Eurocentric whiteness, which has always involved the intersections of class and gender, has denoted itself as superior to other races, be they white or not. Races and cultures by which they are identified.

This is hugely important, as when we talk about constructs of race; we also have to factor in those experiences of racism and racial hatred have been going on against a substantial number of peoples, for a good portion of European, and now Global Northern history. The social constructionist nature of these racialised building blocks will have inevitably played a role within so many of all our intersecting identities. This therefore means that when we encounter experiences of racism, to say that this does not exist denies the literal, cultural, political, religious fabrics that have underpinned Global Northern cultures for hundreds of years.

The religious and political de-humanisation of one group by another, in order to enslave, exploit, and make money out of them, has within it massive levels of racism. Yet, if we move forward from the macro towards the micro, let's say the middle, then what we have is things like race science, things like gentrification, things like redlining – examples of social structures which underpin the systemic structures which we all inhabit, structures that marginalise other groups based upon their difference, their race and their outsiderness. This is the reason behind Figure 2.1 for this section titled 'Intersections of racism', where we start to look at the diverse ways in which racism occurs within a supremacist environment.

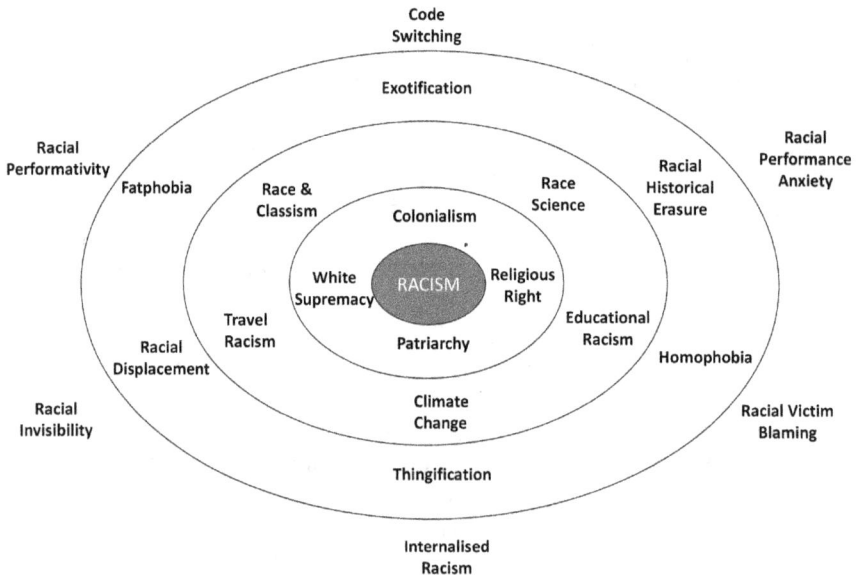

Figure 2.1 Impacts of racism

When we consider Figure 2.1, we have to look at all the separate ways and areas in which racism occurs. Before we get to this point though, it is important to recognise the interlocking intersectional layers of classism, patriarchy, colonialism, white supremacy, and capitalism, which all require levels of inequality and difference in order for them to survive.

The next thing to spot in Figure 2.1 is that in this diagram we move from the systemic to the interpersonal to the internalised aspects of racism. *Systemic racism*, or I could have also used *institutional racism*, involves the way in which institutions, be they political or capitalist or otherwise, were either formed out of forms of racism or have rules that actually reinforce racist views and ideas. *Interpersonal racism* is as it says. As I have already stated in the very first chapter, racism is a relational experience so, not only does it occur between a system or institution and an individual or a group, it will also occur from individual to individual or from one group towards another group or individual. When we consider levels of interpersonal racism, these ways that we might experience racism are often no less subtle and no more destructive than those from the systemic level above it.

The next think to recognise here is *internalised racism*. When we consider internalisation, Hall (1990) recognises that any experience of racism or any sort of performance of racism, be it through the media for example, will inevitably be absorbed by the masses and the individuals. For example, the witnessing of the Black & White Minstrel Show as a child, where you had white performers wearing black face with big white lips to perform old songs, whilst performed on the BBC between the 1950s and the 1970s, and seen to be something of a British institution of the time, often led to levels of mimicry by white counterparts in schools up and down the country, including my own, and levels of shame and grief as endured by myself and many others who were on the receiving end of being called a Gollywog or worse (Hendy, 2023). Internalisations of media racism therefore reinforce the fascist views of a system, or a culture, of a group or institution, and play themselves out both interpersonally and are then internalised by the individuals accordingly.

The next thing to state here is that Figure 2.1 is not a hierarchy. All I am trying to show here is the ways in which the intersecting systems of oppression at the centre, in their desire and need to maintain their levels of power and separation, actually use the psychological supremacy of whiteness over otherness to reinforce said ideals and create and re-create over and over again separations based around racism.

So, when we look at something like the murder of George Floyd as has already been discussed in this book, what we also have to recognise is that his case was one of institutional racism, whereby the Minneapolis police objectified and stereotyped a large, black man based around the idea that he was a possible threat, and thereby murdered him (Various, 2020). But, when they were charged with his murder, the system then took over and initially had them exonerated for these crimes against another human being. The difficulty with this moment, and its performance and sitting on television, social media, and so on, is that it raised to the surface the institutional and cultural levels of racism hidden within companies, organisations, and countries across the world (Various, 2021). What we started to see as well was that on interpersonal levels there was a lot of hate for George Floyd, a lot of anger towards the Black Lives Matter movement, and anger that plenty of people had not realised was present, even if they suspected as much beforehand.

The next layer of this, with a number of persons of difference, be they of colour or allies, was they often saw their own complicity in the adherence and their being wedded to racist stereotypes about George Floyd and many other persons of colour. This, though, also included persons of colour themselves who recognised that they had allowed themselves to be co-opted and coerced into silence around their racial identity, so that when they did so, and when they were met by, in many cases including my own, instances of overt racism designed to actually (re)silence and put the racialised other down, they realised how unsafe they actually were. So, the internalisations always play a part in this racist experience, as does the interpersonal nature of racism, as does the institutional and systemic layer as well.

To offer you some examples from these differing layers, on this occasion I am going to start towards the outside and work inwards. There is one thing I should say before I start running through some of these examples, and that is that this is not exhaustive. There are many different ways that we might experience racism, but what I am trying to do in this example, in this table, in this book, is say and prove that racism is a far more insidious event than those who believe it does not exist would have you believe.

The first instance of racism to notice is *Racial Performance*. Lincoln Theodore Monroe Andrew Perry, born 30 May 1902 and who died on 19 November 1985, was better known by the name Stepin Fetchit. He was an American Vaudevillian comedian and a film actor, who was from Jamaican and Bahamian descent. He was also the first Black actor to have a successful film career in the United States of America. The interesting part though, about this man's career was that in order for him to become famous, he had to engage in what was termed at the time as 'shuckin' and jivin''. The term 'shuckin' and jivin'' had its roots in the times of slavery and was based around performance. This was a means by which slaves on plantations across the Americas and the Caribbean could dance and play and be seen as harmless in front of their white overseers and masters.

Other ways in which this adaptation of blackness occurred include the adaptation of Capoeira, the Brazilian martial art that was banned in Brazil by the Portuguese who saw it as a threat to their power and authority during Portuguese colonialism. The brilliance of this martial art was that this was still performed and adapted into a form of dance by the Africans and the First Nations who lived in Brazil at the time (Almeida, 1986; Kingsford-Smith, 2014). These adaptations, the performance element, are what I mean by racial performance. The idea of performance is in some ways a similar construct to that advocated for by feminists, including Judith Butler, who saw it as a way of being seen as inoffensive and also as desirable under the male gaze (Butler, 1988). For racial performance though, the importance of the term is that it highlights the ability of the racialised other to perform a service of some type which will make them useful to, and safe from, the hatred of those with systemic power.

Racial performance, though, has a deep psychological wounding that goes with it. The inauthenticity of that need to racially adapt to one's circumstances can play out in many other ways, but what it also involves from a psychological perspective is the splitting off and the murdering and killing off of that which makes oneself the other, as posed by the majority (Turner, 2021).

Following on from racial performativity comes its opposite in many ways, *racial performance anxiety*. These are very different experiences and yet have similar beginnings. For racial performativity, the message that people of colour are often given from a very early age is that they are not supposed to show off, they are not supposed to appear too gregarious or to bring shame upon their family or friends (Wigger, 2010). The idea therefore being that one has to conform to a way of being, a way of performing that actually fits in with the black cultural narrative in a white world.

This is also the start point for racial performance anxiety. When asked, for example, many years ago to give a talk to a group of white students on issues of race and difference, the levels of anxiety and fear that wracked my whole body were immense. It therefore took a long time for me to find the courage to say what I needed to say and express myself. Racial performance anxiety involves a person of colour stepping outside of the script passed on to them through childhood and internalised, a script which plays a massive role in the super-egoic sense of self, that part of oneself which from a racialised perspective actually holds sway on our ego and creates the racialised aspect of our false self (R. A. Johnson, 1993).

It is therefore very difficult for persons of colour to have a voice, in a way which is very different to that of a white European woman. I remember at an online event that I hosted back in 2023 how nervous I was during the day or during the morning in the run up to said event. These experiences mean that I have learned to build rituals, both before and afterwards, into any sort of experience like these which allow me to relax, contemplate, meditate, and stay within myself, so I can find the courage to do the work that I need to do. Then, post said events, these rituals are also designed to bring me back down from the highs that I may have encountered and to help ground me back in myself once again.

The relational aspect of this is often there as well. There are an increasing number of persons from the subject group, those who hold opinions opposite to my own, who have found their ways into my talks and presentations. Yet, whilst it is my job to allow them the space to speak up, what often happens is that their need to see themselves as superior, nay as racially superior, and to advocate for the role of whiteness, both as being superior or as more in need of support than any other racialised group, is often present. The fear of the subject to see the racialised other as anything other than the subservient script that is placed upon it, is also part of this performance anxiety and in many ways many of these experiences of racism, because they are relational, are often held within the binary. So, racialised performance anxiety, although presumed to be just about otherness, is often actually about the relationship between the racialised other and the subject whiteness.

The next aspect that I would like to explore here follows on from this in a slightly indirect way, and that is *racial invisibility*. One of the safest ways for the racialised other to meander their way through life and through a world which is not their own, is by remaining invisible. This is not a literal thing because ultimately at any point one might turn a corner, walk towards somebody and be beaten down, have their day disturbed, or be murdered for just being the racialised other. Yet, there are ways in which, by code switching, by performing, by acting in ways which make us appear less aggressive, we also make ourselves more invisible. These experiences are often most pronounced when the opposite happens, through something which has happened in the world which raises the spectre of racism and hatred. So, those of us who have made ourselves invisible in subject spaces, have often found that invisibility, that cloak no longer works for us. In these moments we are exposed, made to sit in front of our peers, a group or whoever, and express what it might be to be that oppressed group who is at war, whose members have been killed by the police, or some other such incident. In 2023 in Israel, because the war and the fear and lived experiences of antisemitism have led so many Jews to hide their identities for fear of hatred across the world, is one sadly recent experience of racial invisibility (Garcia-Navaro, 2023).

Racial invisibility is an adaptation. It is a way for us to actually survive and move beyond and maybe temporarily ignore the fear that we have embedded within ourselves of the hatred embedded within the subject.

Placed along all of these is *code switching* which in a way is a more modern version of racial performance. Code switching (Boulton, 2016) is a term coined by psychologists who recognised that persons of racial difference will often adapt and change the ways in which they act in white environments. This, in more modern parlance, can involve the removal of the base from one's speech, the change in mannerisms from using more patois, to reverting to speaking 'the Queen's English'. It can involve the changing of one's name so one fits into white environments, or it can involve the changing of how one dresses in order to be seen as acceptable within the colonial project.

Several years ago, I wrote a blog based around the colonisation of clothing which in some ways holds elements of code switching (Turner, 2022a). The idea in that blog was that in order to be seen as civilised, as worthy, and as acceptable within a colonised, capitalist, patriarchal framework, one had to dress and act and speak as if one actually belonged (Rovine & Rovine, 2018). Stories abound, for example, of those from the Windrush generation who would wear their best suits, ties, hats, shoes, when they came to the United Kingdom or to Europe, in order to immediately be seen as British, because this is what they had been taught in their own colonised schools and environments. The idea therefore being that within a colonised relationship, in order to be seen as accepted by the coloniser, one had to shed the savagery of the skirt, or the speech, or the ways which set one apart from their more mature, more civilised, more intellectual counterparts and experts.

In many ways, these examples still occur today. The propensity of children of colour or of difference who are castigated for their hair being too nappy, or too kinky, or being labelled in some way, has its roots in the colonial project (Le Roux & Oyedemi, 2023; Leonardo, 2004; Willson, 2021). The idea that hair has to be a certain way for persons of colour automatically marks them out as outsiders, given that these rules were established a very long time ago, but it also becomes a very easy way for those who hold colonised or racist narratives to actually denigrate the racialised other.

It is worth here presenting a more recent example of code switching in this story of Hilton. Hilton was the son of Jewish immigrants from Estonia, who moved to Edinburgh and changed their names in an attempt to settle in and hide their difference after the Second World War. Hilton said of his experience that:

'I'm Jewish, but there is no particular indicator that I'm Jewish; my name is not Jewish, my family, because my father's family changed their name to an anglicised or Scottish name, and I don't look particularly Jewish, and I wasn't brought up within that religion anyway, I was brought up effectively as an atheist. My father's family came to this country from Estonia, and they settled around 1946 and they changed their name around the Second World War, when there was a lot of prejudice against foreigners, so they changed it to a name that I think the idea was that they changed their name to a Scottish name as they didn't want to be associated with being English, because then they would have to explain where they came from. Whereas if they were Scottish, they didn't necessarily have to. They were businesspeople in Edinburgh so they did it for purely practical reasons then. But again, it was because of prejudice, and people were prejudiced against them.'

The code switching is obvious in Hilton's story, as he clearly acknowledges that this was a move his parents made in an attempt to avoid the prejudices of the time. It's also interesting to note the fear of being seen as British is also apparent here, so a type of double code switching.

Moving further inward, we have areas in which racism occurs which may sit within either the interpersonal or the internalised camps. As I should re-state, no one of these areas is completely separate to any other. In fact, what happens is, much like a pebble falling into the middle of a lake, the systemic and institutional influences of racism rippled outwards through the systemic, the institutional, to the individual and then to the internalised, meaning that it is very difficult not to be impacted by the racism embedded within the institutions at the very centre. Examples of this come out of *racial victim blaming*.

At the time of writing this book, it is several years since the murder of George Floyd. In May 2020, during a period whereby most of the planet was under some form of lockdown during the Covid-19 pandemic, George Floyd was murdered on the streets of Minneapolis by several policemen of differing cultures and backgrounds (Various, 2020). The outpouring of distress and anger at seeing yet again on film, on social media, the death of another Black man led to a number of organisations, of peoples, of countries standing up and speaking out against the racial subjugation of Black persons in America.

For this text, the interesting part, though, when it comes to *racial victim blaming*, is the sheer number of people who sought out ways and means by which they could blame the death, nay murder, of a Black man upon his own inability to live a whiter than white life (and yes I have chosen to use those last few words for a reason). Racial victim blaming, simply put, is the means by which white supremacy divests itself of the impact of the racism it has meted out against the racialised other. It is something which is not new and has been used to oppress many minorities such as traveller communities, those from the Jewish culture, and persons of colour across the world. The fact that Floyd may have had a previous criminal record, or that he may have actually had a fake $20 note, should not be the reason or the justification for the murder of a racialised other.

Racial victim blaming also holds within itself aspects of white sympathy, whereby were the same circumstances and situations to be encountered by somebody who was white and male, then the odds are that that person would be treated vastly differently to the person of colour or of difference (Pals, 2021). A difference in treatment based around the fact that they are seen as racially less worthy of respect and gratitude than those who see themselves as white and have power.

Racial victim blaming also runs in other areas of life. In the over-reliance of quality decisions in the United Kingdom where stop and searches are prevalent in certain communities. There is an ideology behind this which holds slivers of racial victim blaming, the fact that we are only stopping you because you are of colour and because you may well be carrying something illegal, then becomes the justification for the repeated harassment of certain communities. This is not just in the United Kingdom, but of racialised minorities in America, in Australia, across Europe and other areas as well. Many of these are driven by the need to oppress the other and have a racialised element within them.

Whitesplaining is another one which is fascinating to witness. No different in a way to mansplaining, whereby within a patriarchal society, as soon as a woman speaks up and says something of worth and of credit, the first thing that a man does, who is normally white, is to explain why their ideas are wrong, detrimental, and should not be seen or heard. Whitesplaining follows a similar path but just alongside a racialised edge.

Dr David Olusoga in 2023 gave a talk as part of the Brighton Festival which was broadcast online. The talk was about many things, with one part being about racism. At the end of what was quite an engaging talk, the first person to speak up and ask not so much a question but to deliver a counterpointed argument, was a white person, male, who felt the need to express himself for a number of minutes; taking up a lot of space before they were finally contained and, in some ways, cut off. Olusoga managed to maintain his cool and continue with the conversation accordingly.

This is whitesplaining. It involves a person without the knowledge, or without the experience, or without the self-awareness, who is obviously triggered by the mere fact that somebody who is non-white chooses to speak up about an area that they themselves have studied for a number of years and have talked about extensively (V. E. Johnson et al., 2021). This means, for this white man in this example, that their unawareness of how embedded within the script of supremacy, of patriarchal and white supremacy they in fact were, led them to become a counterpoint to the argument presented. So, they did not have to sit with their own sense of systemic inferiority.

I myself have had numerous occasions where I have given talks or presentations; at one such presentation, after I had spoken for an hour and a half about a topic, there was an incident whereby, at the end, a white middle class woman decided to label me with anything she could from the left side of the political divide, saying that my ideas were socialist, that those who were oppressed most of all were young, white men, and that most of the people at the talk were afraid to actually speak up and that she was going to stand up for them.

The interesting thing about this is not that I needed to react to it. In a similar vein to Olusoga, he chose not to react to the internalised supremacist's needs of the other person. It feels more just to hold that actually this person in that moment is in pain. There is a script here which has been disturbed – a script of supremacy that sits at the very top, influenced by those who identify as white and who see themselves as superior, at a very deep psychological level, and allows them to actually truly believe and to inculcate the idea that they are better.

The most bizarre example I have ever come across in my own experience occurred after an interview I had published through BACP's *Therapy Today*. In a letter that I received a few weeks afterwards from somebody I had not seen for a number of years, this person stated that whilst they were very happy for me that I had found my way forward and that I was now an established psychotherapist doing some interesting work, they were surprised because they had always seen themselves as my intellectual superior. This person, white, female, middle class, had not only decided that she had a right to have that opinion about me, and that hierarchy, but also felt that she had the right to tell me in an email after so many years that that was how she felt. Whitesplaining therefore sits alongside some of these others in these hierarchies that differentiate one group over another. When we encounter experiences of racism, the power dynamics therefore embedded within them cannot really be denied.

One of the more obscure but interesting cases comes in the guise of *fatphobia*. In a recent piece of research that I myself had done for this book, it became apparent that actually body image ideas, as established by the white patriarchy a couple of hundred years ago, changed over a period of time, whereby persons of colour, who had been enslaved or colonised, were seen as more savage because they were more voluptuous and Rubenesque (Stoll, 2019).

My choice of the phrase Rubenesque is important here because this was no different to the more curvaceous sort of characters and images seen in pictures and paintings dating back to the renaissance and to the work of Peter Paul Rubens. The shift to women having to present themselves as slimmer, as less voluptuous, as less curvaceous, and its subsequent impact on female body image, has its roots in racism meted out against persons of colour. So, when we look at and when we consider just how deeply some of these ideas go, although they are not all going to be just about the patriarchy, people need to recognise that actually so many of these have their links not just in patriarchal narratives but also in white supremacist and capitalist, colonial ideas of specialness. To be thin in this culture is to be seen as civilised.

Another interesting version of this is actually hidden within the song 'Baby's Got Back' by Sir Mix-a-Lot, a New York rapper who produced a top selling single back in the 1980s about his preference for women who were voluptuous and had curves (Sir-Mix-A-Lot, 1992). This was a song which actually appeared on an episode of *Friends*, where one of the characters states her consternation that her baby will only fall asleep to a song which glorified the sexualisation of women through their voluptuousness (Halvorson, 2002). It is important to recognise the strong racialised message hidden within 'Baby's Got Back' alongside the colonial message hidden within the character's words in *Friends*, when we start to explore the idea that actually this is a culture whereby curves or, more importantly, the natural body of plenty of women, is not seen as desirable or acceptable within a colonial narrative.

Moving to *racial historical erasure*, this is as it says. Building on the idea of historical erasure, the moulding of a narrative by the colonisers, or by those with systemic power, a narrative which then marginalises the influences of or crimes against the other, is a common facet of supremacy (Berger, 2022; Hunt, 2017). Examples of racial erasure come from many areas. For example, the marginalisation and erasure of feminists of colour from mainstream feminism, is something oft debated within feminist discourse (Montiel Valle & Martin, 2021; Verges, 2021).

When we consider the fuller experiences of racial historical erasure, stories abound of the impact of persons of colour, of those who are Jewish, Islamic, or of other faiths, and their influences upon cultures of the Global North. The erasures, multiple, of their influences, their inventions, and impacts upon the lives of all of us, is one of the largest historical travesties of our times. The means behind this being one to propagate the myths of white, patriarchal, colonialist superiority, by denying the influences of so many people from the racialised other.

As we start to move slightly further inwards and access areas which have a strong interpersonal message but are also very much driven by institutions and systemic narratives, perhaps more so than some of the others towards the bottom, an interesting place to start is in *racial homophobia*. In Uganda in 2023 a law was passed which banned LGBTQ individuals from overtly expressing their sexuality. In this move, a movement echoed in a number of formerly colonised countries, there is also an increased level of fear for those minorities who are identified as the racialised other. The roots of much of this are actually within colonialism but also hold ties to patriarchal or male superiority and white supremacy (Kizito, 2017; Onyulo, 2017). The fact that these scripts also tie themselves to religious aspects is not lost upon myself but again this is a part of the book that I cannot cover here because it deserves its own narrative – how the use of religion has led to the oppression of many different groups for hundreds of years (Various, 2010).

Racial homophobia is something which also sits within varying minority groups. The fear of LGBTQ persons of colour across the Global North means that it is often not safe for them to be seen as active, as present within their own environments, within their own cultures (Aosved et al., 2009; Bachmann & Gooch, 2017). In the final series of *Sex Education* as broadcast on Netflix (Various, n.d.), the journey that Eric, play by Ncuti Gatwa, in owning his own sexuality whilst trying to negotiate his religious and cultural background, is an emotional and important part of the story. It also highlights clearly and eloquently, the levels of internalised racism that sit within a group, a culture that was not there before.

The next area to consider I have actually given two titles. The first one is *racial displacement* but it also could go under the title of *racial punching down*. The reasons for this are fairly obvious once explained in this text. Displacement is a term used within the world of psychodynamic psychotherapy (Adey, 2020). This is a process which begins with a client's, or an individual's, need to see themselves as well enough, as capable enough, as competent enough, even when there is obvious evidence to the contrary. In order for this self-belief to be made true, what they will do is displace any sort of feelings of lack of worth, or any sort of self-hatred onto another group (Luci, 2020). *Racial displacement* is constructed out of a similar narrative. What this actually means though is that certain cultures, where they believe themselves as better than, or superior to, other cultures, will displace any sort of feelings of lack of worth onto their contemporaries, normally using racial difference as a gateway to said psychological projection. The ultimate goal of racial displacement is to maintain the hierarchical nature of racism, moving away from the interdependent nature of the racial construct.

This can even happen within a racial grouping. In the acclaimed *Small Island*, by Andrea Levy (2009), the author utilises a title based around the arguments, discussions, and put downs Caribbean nations would often have based around their homelands. The *Small Island* argument holds the idea that those who are from the larger Caribbean islands of say Jamaica or Cuba would look down upon others from other Afro-Caribbean islands, such as Antigua, Barbados, and Trinidad. In my own family, one of the more constant arguments that would go on would be between my father, a Jamaican, and my mother a Trinidadian, and was always based around which island was larger, and therefore superior, meaning who was better and conversely who was inferior.

When we factor in the idea of *racial punching down*, what we also to see though is a form of hierarchy. Within a racialised system, a system based within the idea that whiteness is superior to Blackness, racialised displacement and racialised punching down will always involve a continuation of said hierarchy, whereby nobody wants to live on the bottom rung of a society. This is no different to class-based displacement whereby, from a political perspective, the working classes are often manipulated by those from the middle and upper classes to see immigrants as less than them and as the other (Herk et al., 2011). Or, in certain communities, where there are class-based narratives whereby certain members of working class communities will always see themselves as superior to others from the same community and often the same environment and same road, based upon where they live on the road, how many children they have, the work that they do, or do not do, and their general standing within said community. Hierarchies are a massive part of the racialised punching down and the racialised displacement.

The reason this is a form of racism is because it stretches away from the more community-based ways of living embedded deep within the histories of plenty of persons of racial difference. The hierarchical nature of whiteness when internalised therefore means that persons of racialised otherness create other hierarchies within their own groups, and even unconsciously within themselves. Within the more afro-centric cultures, for example within the spirit of Ubuntu, the idea of a hierarchy does not exist in anywhere near the same way. The idea that one knows oneself based around one's relationship to the other suggests that we are all interconnected, be it as people, as creatures on this planet, or even with the planet itself (Hailey, 2008). The hierarchy then does not really exist. Our experience, our way of living and how we live becomes a joint collective experience where we live together and we die together. The hierarchy, the race to superiority, is straight out of the Darwinian idea of survival of the fittest and is very much a Eurocentric idea of how we form our identity. Given the perspectives that we have all inculcated, it is obvious therefore that persons of colour will have taken on board this need to be seen as superior, or more importantly, not to be seen as less than (Hall, 1990).

My own parents, when they arrived in the United Kingdom, saw themselves as English, as part of the Empire and, in many ways, they believed they were citizens of the United Kingdom. Yet, when they arrived here, they were immediately met with that sense that they were less than, that they were the other, that they were not the same as their white counterparts within this country. Their ways of managing this were to bond with other persons from other islands, build their own communities, and band together but there were also other, more subtle ways, which were utilised to actually reinforce a sense of superiority.

So, those who then travelled to the United Kingdom from the Caribbean or from other parts of the colonised world, and yet who had not been raised in a time of colonialism, were often seen as being less than, as being unable to relate and to speak the Queen's English and not capable or able to present themselves as British enough. There was a sense that they were inferior to those of my parents' generation, for example, in some instances, but not necessarily in all.

Alongside this, when plenty of the Windrush generation travelled back to the Caribbean, they were often seen by those left behind as being English, British, given nicknames as such and seen as such. This being because they were held to a different standard to those still living in the West Indies. This racialised hierarchy holds within it forms of punching down and displacement, both up and down, and is therefore a concept created outside of the phenomenology of racism.

The next pair are some areas of racism that I have covered before in varying texts. The first one of these is the exotification of the racialised other. *Exotification* is a term used to denote the sexualisation of persons of colour, persons of difference, based around characteristics, nay stereotypes based around how they present (Andersen, 2014; Turner, 2023). Obvious examples come from the sexualisation of adults of colour based round their curvature, their shape, or their physical and sexual attributes.

In a blog post written by myself some years ago, I wrote about the sexualisation of Black men by not just white women, or European women, but also by men as well, and how the levels of racism held within that have led to the exotification of Blackness (Turner, 2022b, 2022c). In the earliest example I gave in this book of the woman who just wanted to know whether it was true about Black men, the fact that her vision of Blackness was based around whether a Black man was well hung or not, was and is nothing new.

Cuckolding is a concept and a practice used within certain couples, whereby a man and a woman will play with the power dynamics in their relationship by inviting in another person, normally a man, to perform some sexual acts upon a woman whilst her partner watches and gains some sort of sexualised satisfaction from this form of ritualised humiliation (Lehmiller et al., 2018; Pavlovic & Pavlovic, 2012). Racialised cuckolding carries on in the same vein and yet within that there is also the preponderance and the activation of that racialised stereotypical element which adds an extra frisson to the whole experience for said white couple (Miller-Young & Livermon, 2019).

The sexualisation of Black women is something which also goes back to the times of slavery and colonialism. As already expressed in fatphobia and its racist element, the idea that a woman of colour with curves and with shape was therefore seen as more savage, did not prevent a good number of men and some women from sexualising and abusing women of colour for generations (Akbar, 1984). This racism element to how women of colour are often viewed and the marginalising of the shapes of women of colour actually made them more desirable for those men of power, or men of whiteness, who therefore believed that this is what they needed to have – their intent being to break said socially constructed taboo in order to achieve and relieve themselves of this sense of pious superiority, at least temporarily.

This exotification can also become internalised within the racialised other, whereby persons of racialised difference may well play up to and embrace that exotified persona in order to achieve a level of racialised superiority within a white framework, whilst also distancing themselves from their true racial kin.

Thingification is a term which I used in the book *The Psychology of Supremacy* (Turner, 2023) and talks about the objectification of the racialised other in order for other forms of abuse and use to be utilised against them or it. Thingification was a phrase created by Aime Cesaire (2000) and is something which we can actually do to ourselves when internalised. In many ways, when we talk about things such as *code switching* or the *racialised performance* as mentioned earlier in this chapter, there is a thingification of our own authentic identity which is the racism of whiteness internalised.

The other part to this is that we can also thingify ourselves in order to find a level of safety within majority spaces. This has ties to something called minority stress, whereby whenever a person of colour, in this instance, walks into an environment, there is always the underlying anticipation of an experience of racism, marginalisation, and exotification (Feinstein et al., 2012; Flanders et al., 2016). That stressful, hyper-alertness can often be met with, and countered by, moments whereby we thingify ourselves as a way of creating safety, either by finding safety in groups, or by making ourselves less threatening in order to create safety in the face of racialised subjects.

Looking at areas such as education, in a wonderful set of films directed by Steve McQueen, there was one in particular called *Small Axe: Education* (McQueen, 2020). This film looked at the ways in which the first generation of non-white immigrants were treated to a lower standard of education than their white counterparts. There was a general stereotypical feeling in this particular film that those who identified as the racialised other were less intelligent and in some ways substandard. Their educational path therefore being one of being marginalised and put into special schools. These systems of racism within the educational system have not in any way ended since the 1960s and 1970s. In fact in the current era, when we consider university attainment gaps, although there are increased numbers of persons of colour and the racialised other taking up university places, the attainment gaps between non-white and white students is vastly different by an average of 16 percentage points (Bhopal et al., 2018; Various, 2019).

This is indicative, I would suggest, of the institutional and systemic levels of racism that sit within our cultures in the Global North. The propensity for racism within the educational system and the denial of its existence by the system itself, whilst also being met with the obvious stats and figures which say otherwise, speaks an awful lot of how the system and the institutions reconstitute their levels of inequality. The next layer is how this then impacts upon the racialised other when they look to obtain jobs post qualifying.

In fact, I was given a story by a colleague of colour, Reggie, who was raised in Scandinavia to African/Norwegian parents:

> Although Reggie encountered a great deal of racism in his schooling, he did manage to do well enough to get himself to university where he succeeded in his aims in getting a good degree. He spoke often of how difficult it was in the 1970s in Europe to find a place of safety within educational establishments, so much so that he was ultimately relieved to have achieved such a good grade and standard in his final assessments at university. When he entered the jobs market though, he was met by another systemic and institutional layer of racism, whereby on more than one occasion he was told that although he was well enough qualified for the positions which he was applying for, they would not hire him because no one would want to work under a N*****. This led to him ultimately becoming quite disillusioned with the racism inbuilt within the system, the institution and the individuals that he was encountering, so much so that he ended up working for himself ultimately, whilst falling into periods of depression and substance misuse.

The ongoing impact of racism in the educational system does not end when a person leaves the educational environment. I remember from my own process in therapy having to spend a great deal of time working with my therapist to find my voice, to realise that the imposter syndrome which I had internalised was very much built out of my experiences in a secondary school that marginalised Black people. So much so, that my becoming a doctor was something which I encountered and achieved quite late in life. Even though I had performed quite well at primary school, by the time I went to a private secondary school I found the change of environment and the systemic racism embedded within it to be quite difficult to deal with and manage.

Healthcare is a fascinating and disturbing area which also holds within it racist undertones. From the measuring of skulls in a form of scientific racism which was designed to denote the intelligence, or lack of, of the racialised other, this is another example of how medicine and science, in their collision, have actually underpinned and re-emphasised some of the racism against other groupings (Saini, 2019). Slaves who were deemed to have the mental illness, drapetomania, were diagnosed because they did not uphold their natural position as slaves for whiteness, is another shocking example (Willoughby, 2018).

More recent perspectives have often been flagged up in the huge disparities between rates of illness or death of the privileged and the racialised others in the modern era. Perfect examples include the disparate rates of illness and death for the racialised other during Covid-19, and the fact that there are five times as many women of colour who die during childbirth as there are those who are white (British Psychological Society, 2020).

This continued sacrificial lambing of the racialised other in service to systemic and institutional whiteness within healthcare and the scientific world also highlights just how deeply embedded racism actually is. In working alongside a number of colleagues and friends, some of whom are midwives, they mentioned with some consternation how much of the training that they received and the teaching that they underwent involved looking at things through not only a very patriarchal lens but also one which was very white. They also noted that this lens marginalised other areas of concern for women such as the menopause or endometriosis and other illnesses which inhibit a sizeable number of women on the planet. They also recognised that they were ill-prepared for the levels and types of needs for women of the racialised other to the extent that they would often have to spend a lot more time exploring and investigating what those needs might involve and how they might best address them.

Looking at travel, we have all seen images from brochures and adverts of people flying off to exotic climes, such as The Maldives or America, or Fiji. What we often see in these images though is two things: first, the very sanitised versions of these environments and places presented as an ideal that that person, that customer may wish to have, were they to have enough money. Then, secondly, that certain areas of the world, certain climes and environments are often seen as better places to go for persons of whiteness than for others (Benjamin & Dillette, 2021; Li et al., 2020). When it comes to images of say Africa, or even parts of Asia and India, what we are often presented with is the opposite. It is the deprivation, the isolation, the poverty, the famines, the war, as per the media representations, and we are often left bereft of images of the white sandy beaches of Zanzibar, the rolling sand dunes of Namibia, or the rolling green planes of Zambia, and the beauty of Victoria Falls.

It often falls to the racialised other to find their own way and their own route through exploring beyond the racialised stereotypes of their own lands, in their connection and reconnection to areas that they know full well that are not as presented in mainstream Global Northern media.

I remember working with a transpersonal facilitator some years ago, right before I was due to take my umpteenth trip to Africa, who said to me, 'You are very brave to be going there, I'm not sure how I would cope with going somewhere which is so threatening and alien to me.' The fact that I did not have the time to actually challenge her narrative was more down to the fact that we had workshops to go and run. Yet, it has always stayed with me, knowing that this was a person who I knew full well had travelled a great deal to parts of India and so on, had done so from a place of colonial privilege. So, to therefore engage with Africa would probably mean that she would do so from that same level of superiority. Whereas, for somebody like myself staying in a YMCA in the middle of Darussalam was actually quite a wonderful way for me just to be in and amongst people who are similar to myself.

The climate crisis is another one on this list of ways in which racism will and has appeared. We are already seeing, as the climate emergency rolls ever onwards and towards us and through us, the disparities in approaches between the rich nations of the Global North and the poorer and increasingly desperate nations of the rest of the world (Ares, 2021). The incredible presentation given by Philip Davis, President of the Bahamas back in 2022 at a climate change conference about the horrors about to be meted against his own country in the face of rising waters and how it was met by such apathy by the richer nations of the Global North is a shocking, but not uncommon indictment of the lack of interest and care the richer nations have paid towards those who are most impacted by rising sea levels and global warming (P. Davis, 2022). The ability to deny even the existence of such an existential horror holds within itself aspects of privilege and entitlement in the face of scientific rigour and knowledge, the arrogance of which underpins the hatred of the racialised other (Deivanayagam et al., 2023; Mathers, 2022). But even more individual experiences of the impact of climate change should not be underestimated.

In January 2023, David Lammy, the Shadow Foreign Secretary gave a speech on Foreign Policy at Chatham House. During this speech, Mr Lammy spoke about Ella Kissi-Debrah. Ella was a nine-year-old girl from Southeast London, who was killed, in part, by the unlawful levels of air pollution near her home. The fact that racism and housing and climate change are all part of this young girl's death and experience should be something which brings shame to us all, and yet it is often not considered because there is a lack of care and respect paid towards someone so young, a racialised other in her infancy. So many of the areas we have considered here sit under the umbrella of classism, patriarchy, colonialism, white supremacy, and capitalism because all of these, all parts of this umbrella in their own ways play roles in the formation and the manipulation and the ongoing systems of racism which float around us all the time. So, and whilst this chart is in no way exhaustive, what it does start to do is look at how racism is far more complex and far more widespread than the oft political naysayers of its existence would ever have you believe.

The *white-washing of racism*, a phrase invented by myself, speaks a lot of the ability of those who see themselves as superior and without shame, to deny the existence of racism, even when presented with so many examples such as these. For those on the opposite end who identify as the racialised other, irrespective of whether they are Roma, Jewish, of colour, or otherwise, I invite them all to explore within themselves, or in their groups, or on their training courses, the other ways in which racism may actually appear. I say this because this is not a book which looks to definitely define racism – it is a book which looks to explore, uncover, or even reveal, aspects of phenomenological racism to which we can all add our own experiences because, ultimately, we are all moulded by systems of phenomenological racism.

Summary

As detailed here in Figure 2.1, there are a sizeable number of ways in which racism can be experienced, all of which are driven by the religious right, patriarchy, white supremacy, and capitalism. To therefore suggest that racism does not exist is therefore also to deny the numerous ways in which we walk with it all of the time. In some ways, I wonder if that ability for the subject to deny racism's existence is in part because of the privileges embedded within all these sorts of experiences for the subject in relationship to the racialised other.

Yes, racism is a very difficult thing to face and disrupt and part of that is because it is so well embedded within the world that is around us, and therefore within ourselves, every single one of us. The hatred of systemic whiteness towards those who are from Asia during the Covid-19 pandemic, which led to increasing numbers of hate crimes, also dovetails with the anti-Black racism of Asians towards persons of colour, and also dovetails into the anti-Asian hatred meted out by persons of colour towards those who are brought from India to the Caribbean.

This chapter will hopefully allow people to start to explore where they sit within many of the examples I have presented here and maybe where there are some examples that I have not included, for whatever reason that might be. The next pathway in this book, though, is to look at how racism then becomes internalised and how, because race and racism is an artificial social construct, their internalisation runs deep and is actually quite traumatic. The next chapter, entitled *'The Trauma of Racism'* considers not just the embodied impact of racism, but the mental health impact of it as well.

References

Adey, P. (2020). *The handbook of displacement*. Palgrave.
Akbar, N. (1984). *Breaking the chains of psychological slavery*. New Mind.
Almeida, B. (1986). *Capoeira: History, philosophy, practice*. North Atlantic Books.

Andersen, P. D. (2014). The Hollywood beach party genre and the exotification of youthful white masculinity in early 1960s America. *Men and Masculinities, 18*(5), 511–535. https://doi.org/10.1177/1097184X14558880

Andrews, K. (2016). The psychosis of whiteness: The celluloid hallucinations of Amazing Graze and Belle. *Journal of Black Studies*, 1–13. https://doi.org/10.1177/0021934716638802

Andrews, K., & Palmer, L. (2013). Why Black Studies matters. *Discover Society, 2*, 1–4.

Aosved, A. C., Long, P. J., & Voller, E. K. (2009). Measuring sexism, racism, sexual prejudice, ageism, classism, and religious intolerance: The intolerant Schema Measure. *Journal of Applied Social Psychology, 39*(10), 2321–2354. https://doi.org/10.1111/j.1559-1816.2009.00528.x

Ares, E. (2021). COP26: The international climate change conference, Glasgow, UK. *House of Commons Library, October*, 1–21. https://researchbriefings.files.parliament.uk/documents/CBP-8868/CBP-8868.pdf

Bachmann, C. L., & Gooch, B. (2017). *LGBT in Britain: Hate crime and discrimination.* www.stonewall.org.uk/lgbt-britain-hate-crime-and-discrimination

Benjamin, S., & Dillette, A. K. (2021). Black travel movement: Systemic racism informing tourism. *Annals of Tourism Research, 88*, 103169. https://doi.org/10.1016/j.annals.2021.103169

Berger, M. T. (2022). Coining intersectional stigma: Historical erasures and the future. *American Journal of Public Health, 112*, S338–S339. https://doi.org/10.2105/AJPH.2022.306730

Bhopal, K., Pitkin, C., & Hunt, S. (2018). *Investigating higher education institutions and their views on the Race Equality Charter.* Centre for Research in Race in Education, University of Birmingham.

Boulton, C. (2016). Black identities inside advertising: Race inequality, code switching, and stereotype threat. *Howard Journal of Communications, 27*(2), 130–144. https://doi.org/10.1080/10646175.2016.1148646

British Psychological Society. (2020). *DCP Racial and Social Inequalities in the Times of Covid-19 Working Group.*

Butler, J. (1988). Performative acts and gender constitution: An essay in phenomenology and feminist theory. *Theatre Journal, 40*(4), 519. https://doi.org/10.2307/3207893

Cesaire, A. (2000). *Discourse on colonialism.* USA: Monthly Review Press.

Cox, M., & Thielgaard, A. (1986). *Mutative metaphors in psychotherapy: The Aeolian mode.* Tavistock.

Davis, P. (2022). Climate Change and Carbon Markets Initiatives Bill, 2022. *Commonwealth OF THE Bahamas.* www.bahamas.gov.bs/wps/wcm/connect/459fe958-fb82-413b-9229-85535905a3b7/Climate+Change+and+Carbon+Credit+2022.pdf?MOD=AJPERES#:~:text=Honourable Philip "Brave" Davis chose

Deivanayagam, T. A., English, S., Hickel, J., Bonifacio, J., Guinto, R. R., Hill, K. X., Huq, M., Issa, R., & Mulindwa, H. (2023). Health policy envisioning environmental equity: Climate change, health, and racial justice. *The Lancet, 6736*(23). https://doi.org/10.1016/S0140-6736(23)00919-4

Ellis, E. (2021). *The race conversation: An essential guide to creating life-changing dialogue.* Confer Books.

Feinstein, B. a, Goldfried, M. R., & Davila, J. (2012). The relationship between experiences of discrimination and mental health among lesbians and gay men: An examination of internalized homonegativity and rejection sensitivity as potential mechanisms. *Journal of Consulting and Clinical Psychology, 80*(5), 917–927. https://doi.org/10.1037/a0029425

Fernando, F. (2020). *Philosophical posthumanism (Theory in the New Humanities).* Bloomsbury Academic.

Flanders, C. E., Robinson, M., Legge, M. M., & Tarasoff, L. A. (2016). Negative identity experiences of bisexual and other non-monosexual people: A qualitative report. *Journal of Gay & Lesbian Mental Health, 20*, 2–21. https://doi.org/10.1080/19359705.2015.1108257

Garcia-Navaro, L. (2023). *A surge in antisemitism in Europe – and what's behind it. New York Times.* www.nytimes.com/2023/11/02/podcasts/headlines-europe-antisemitism-israel-hamas.html

Hailey, J. (2008). *Ubuntu : A literature review. A paper prepared for the Tutu Foundation* (Issue November).

Hall, S. (1990). Cultural identity and diaspora. In J. Rutherford (Ed.), *Identity: Commodity, Culture, Difference* (pp. 222–237). Lawrence & Wishart.

Halvorson, G. (2002). *The one with Ross's inappropriate song* (p. 1). NBC.

Hegel, G. (1976). *Phenomenology of spirit.* Oxford University Press.

Heidegger, M. (2010). *Being and time.* Suny Press.

Hendy, D. (2023). *The Black and White Minstrel Show.* BBC. www.bbc.com/historyofthebbc/100-voices/people-nation-empire/make-yourself-at-home/the-black-and-white-minstrel-show

Herk, K. A. Van, Smith, D., & Andrew, C. (2011). Examining our privileges and oppressions: Incorporating an intersectionality paradigm into nursing. *Nursing Inquiry, 18*(1), 29–39.

Homer, S. (2007). *Jacques Lacan: Routledge critical thinkers (Kindle Edition).* Routledge.

Hunt, M. R. (2017). The 1689 Mughal Siege of East India company Bombay: Crisis and historical erasure. *History Workshop Journal, 84*(1), 149–169. https://doi.org/10.1093/hwj/dbx034

Husserl, E. (2012). *Ideas: General introduction to pure phenomenology.* Routledge.

Jacobs, M. (2003). *Sigmund Freud: Key figures in counselling and psychotherapy* (2nd ed.). Sage.

Johnson, R. A. (1993). *Owning your own shadow: Understanding the dark side of the psyche.* Harper Collins.

Johnson, V. E., Nadal, K. L., Sissoko, D. R. G., & King, R. (2021). 'It's not in your head': Gaslighting, 'splaining, victim blaming, and other harmful reactions to microaggressions. *Perspectives on Psychological Science, 16*(5), 1024–1036. https://doi.org/10.1177/17456916211011963

Jung, C. G. (1959). *Aion: Researches into the phenomenology of the self* (5th ed.). Princeton University Press.

Kamwangamalu, N. M. (1999). Ubuntu in South Africa: A sociolinguistic perspective to a pan-African concept Ubuntu: A pan-African concept. *Critical Arts, 24*(2), 24–41.

Keeling, D. M., & Lehman, M. N. (2018). Posthumanism. *Oxford Research Encyclopedia of Communication, May,* 1–26. https://doi.org/10.1093/acrefore/9780190228613.013.627

Kingsford-Smith, A. (2014). *Disguised in dance: The secret history of Capoeira.* Brazil : The Best of Its Art and Culture. http://theculturetrip.com/south-america/brazil/articles/disguised-in-dance-the-secret-history-of-capoeira/

Kinouani, G. (2021). *Living while Black: The essential guide to overcoming racial trauma.* Ebury Press.

Kizito, K. (2017). Bequeathed legacies: Colonialism and state-led homophobia in Uganda. *Surveillance and Society, 15*(3–4), 567–572. https://doi.org/10.24908/ss.v15i3/4.6617

Le Roux, J., & Oyedemi, T. D. (2023). Entrenched coloniality? Colonial-born Black Women, hair and identity in post-apartheid South Africa. *African Studies.* https://doi.org/10.1080/00020184.2023.2261387

Lehmiller, J. J., Ley, D., & Savage, D. (2018). The psychology of gay men's cuckolding fantasies. *Archives of Sexual Behavior, 47*(4), 999–1013. https://doi.org/10.1007/s10508-017-1096-0

Leonardo, Z. (2004). The color of supremacy: Beyond the discourse of 'white privilege'. *Educational Philosophy and Theory, 36*(2), 137–152

Levinas, E. (1961). *Totality and infinity: An essay on exteriority.* Duquesne University Press.

Levy, A. (2009). *Small island.* Tinder Press.

Li, S., Li, G., Law, R., & Paradies, Y. (2020). Racism in tourism reviews. *Tourism Management, 80*(July 2019), 104100. https://doi.org/10.1016/j.tourman.2020.104100

Luci, M. (2020). Displacement as trauma and trauma as displacement in the experience of refugees. *Journal of Analytical Psychology, 65*(2), 260–280. https://doi.org/10.1111/1468-5922.12590

Mathers, D. (2022). Climate change and racism: or, why Tarzan can't help us save the planet. *Journal of Analytical Psychology, 67*(5), 1490–1496. https://doi.org/10.1111/1468-5922.12864

McQueen, S. (2020). *Small Axe: Education*. BBC. www.bbc.co.uk/iplayer/episode/m000qfb1/small-axe-series-1-education

Merleau-ponty, M. (1962). *The phenomenology of perception*. Routledge.

Merleau-ponty, M. (2002). *The world of perception*. Routledge.

Miller-Young, M., & Livermon, X. (2019). Black stud, white desire: Black masculinity in cuckold pornography and sex work. In A. D. Davis & B. S. E. Collective (Eds.), *Black sexual economies: Race and sex in a culture of capital*. University of Illinois Press. https://doi.org/10.5622/illinois/9780252042645.003.0003

Moerer-Urdahl, T., & Creswell, J. W. (2004). Using transcendental phenomenology to explore the 'ripple effect' in a leadership mentoring program. *International Journal of Qualitative Studies, 3*(2), 19–35.

Montiel Valle, D. A., & Martin, Z. C. (2021). Entangled with the necropolis: A decolonial feminist analysis of femicide news coverage in Latin America. *Feminist Media Studies, 00*(00), 1–16. https://doi.org/10.1080/14680777.2021.1988675

Neville, H. a, Awad, G. H., Brooks, J. E., Flores, M. P., & Bluemel, J. (2013). Color-blind racial ideology: Theory, training, and measurement implications in psychology. *The American Psychologist, 68*(6), 455–466. https://doi.org/10.1037/a0033282

Onyulo, T. (2017). *Uganda's other refugee crisis: Discrimination forces many LGBT Ugandans to seek asylum*. USA Today. https://eu.usatoday.com/story/news/world/2017/07/13/uganda-other-refugee-crisis-lgbt-ugandanss/475353001/

Pals, A. (2021). *Himpathy? The impact of defendant social status on perceptions of a rape legal case*. University of Kentucky.

Pavlovic, R. Y., & Pavlovic, A. M. (2012). Dostoevsky and psychoanalysis: *The Eternal Husband* (1870) by Fyodor Dostoevsky (1821–1881). *British Journal of Psychiatry, 200*(3), 181–181. https://doi.org/10.1192/bjp.bp.111.093823

Rovine, V. L., & Rovine, V. L. (2018). Colonialism's clothing: Africa, France, and the deployment of fashion. *Design Issues, 25*(3), 44–61.

Saini, A. (2019). *Superior: The return of race science*. Harper Collins.

Sir-Mix-A-Lot. (1992). Baby Got Back. In *Mack Daddy*. Def Jam.

Stein, M. (2005). Individuation: Inner work. *Journal of Jungian Theory and Practice, 7*(2), 1–13.

Stoll, L. C. (2019). Fat is a social justice issue, too. *Humanity & Society, 43*(4), 421–441. https://doi.org/10.1177/0160597619832051

Turner, D. D. L. (2021). *Intersections of privilege and otherness in counselling and psychotherapy* (1st ed.). Routledge.

Turner, D. D. L. (2022a). *#DecoloniseThis I: Clothing and colonialism*. Dwight Turner Counselling. www.dwightturnercounselling.co.uk/2022/04/28/decolonisethis-i-clothing-and-colonialism/

Turner, D. D. L. (2022b). *#DecoloniseThis I: Clothing and colonialism*. Dwight Turner Counselling. www.dwightturnercounselling.co.uk/2022/04/28/decolonisethis-i-clothing-and-colonialism/

Turner, D. D. L. (2022c). *Decolonising Me II: Escaping the homoerotic shackles of the white male gaze*. Dwight Turner Counselling. www.dwightturnercounselling.co.uk/2022/05/30/decolonising-me-ii-escaping-the-homoerotic-shackles-of-the-white-male-gaze/

Turner, D. D. L. (2023). *The psychology of supremacy*. Routledge.

Various. (n.d.). *Sex education*. Netflix. www.imdb.com/title/tt7767422/fullcredits

Various. (2010). *Uganda : Anti-homosexuality bill is inherently discriminatory and threatens broader*. www.amnesty.org/en/wp-content/uploads/2021/06/afr590032010en.pdf

Various. (2019). Bame student attainment. In *National Union of Students*. www.universitiesuk.ac.uk/what-we-do/policy-and-research/publications/black-asian-and-minority-ethnic-student

Various. (2020). *George Floyd death*. BBC News. www.bbc.co.uk/news/topics/cv7wlylxzg1t/george-floyd-death

Various. (2021). *Has George Floyd changed Britain?* ITV. www.itv.com/presscentre/ep1week19/trevor-mcdonald-charlene-white-has-george-floyd-changed-britain#

Verges, F. (2021). *A decolonial feminism*. Pluto Press.

Wigger, I. (2010). 'Black shame': The campaign against 'racial degeneration' and female degradation in interwar Europe. *Race Relations, 51*(3), 33–46. https://doi.org/10.1177/0306396809354444

Willoughby, C. D. E. (2018). Running away from Drapetomania: Samuel A. Cartwright medicine, and race in the antebellum south. *Journal of Southern History, 84*(3), 579–614. https://doi.org/10.1353/soh.2018.0164

Willson, N. (2021). 'I like my baby heir with baby hair and afros': Black majesty and the fault-lines of colonialism. *Women's Studies International Forum, 84*, 1–25.

Chapter 3

The Trauma of Racism

Introduction

I have never been one for getting into any fights. Yet, in my school, the school I had been sent to by my parents who very much wanted me to fit in within this culture, I got into one particular fight which I would like to mention.

At the age of about fourteen, whilst I was walking back to my classroom after lunch, I found myself being picked on by a number of my peers. This was not a one-off, it was not an unusual occurrence, it was a regular thing that happened in a private school in West London. Part of the reason I was picked on was because I was one of only two Black boys in and amongst 150 other children. This was an all-male which meant that we were very much the minority. The fact that we ended up in separate classes for a good amount of our time in that school also added to the sense of feeling very much alone, marginalised and an outsider. So that, whilst I had a good number of friends who were mainly Asian, I was also a lot of the time left to my own devices and, when I was around my peers in my year group and in my class group, often there would be anything from teasing to overt racial comments from the students, things which were not challenged at all by the teachers.

After three years of this treatment, on one particular day, I snapped. A boy found it within himself to find the courage to approach me and call me a racial slur. I pushed him as hard as I possibly could so that this boy, who was about the same height and size as myself, flew across the room, tripping over his feet and banging his head against the skirting board. This of course meant that his head was split open and his peers, the other bullies, who were concerned for his safety, suddenly ran to his side, picked him up and immediately rushed him off to the nurse. I, of course, did not know what to do with myself, realising that I had lashed out in a way that was alien to myself, using an expression of the tension that had built up within myself over a number of years.

We were both inevitably sent to the headmaster's office. The principal on hearing our stories decided that we both needed to be caned. My assailant

DOI: 10.4324/9781003508854-3

received one lash of the cane, whilst I received two because I had lost control of myself, even though I had been provoked.

The importance of this story is not just to show how difficult it is to continually endure the racialised slings and arrows of hatred's fortune, but also to help us start to explore the internalisation and the suppression of the pressure that those who are on the receiving end of racism must often endure.

The psychological impact of racism is something which should not be underestimated. In the previous two chapters, we have looked at just some of the many ways in which racism impacts upon persons of difference, of racialised difference, across the Global North. From historical erasure, to gentrification, to fatphobia, to more obvious examples, all will have an impact upon individuals and groups in ways in which many of us cannot quite understand. In Chapter 2, the presentation of a Jewish client whose parents felt they needed to change their name when arriving in the UK is a facet of that historical self-erasure that goes with a fear of racist incidences towards oneself.

This chapter will therefore take a look at the psychology of racism and how actually, on a developmental level, because we encounter racism so early on in life, we quickly learn to either adapt, rebel, or die, based around the systemic messages which are passed through us. It will explore the psychological and developmental impacts of racism because these I feel are important to fully understand. It will also investigate the mental and embodied impacts of racism because, remember in my initial example for this chapter, the fact that I could not sleep, the fact that I felt sick to the stomach, suggests that experiencing and witnessing racist incidents has a physiological and neurological impact upon those on the receiving end.

So, the second part of this chapter will look at the neuroscience behind the impact of racism. We are also going to look at the health impact of racism; the ways in which persons, communities, try and cope with experiences of racism before also exploring trauma and racism. The important part about this last section of the chapter, which will hopefully bring this all together, is that, as I have tried to state, although racism is a relational event and experience, it is also a traumatic one that can lead persons and groups to find themselves having to find ways to adapt to said experiences.

In order to explore so much of this information, it is therefore important for us to begin with the psychological impact of racism.

The construction of race

One of the strangest aspects of this exploration of race is, given that it is a social construct, where does it emerge from and why? My answer to this means that we need to firstly recognise that culture and envy have become intertwined over generations. What I mean by this is that cultures, be they Sinto, Mesopotamian, or Mayan, have evolved within their own times, and had nothing and no one to compare themselves against – and therefore see themselves as less than. There was often no need, or no desire to do just this. Yet, in other, relatively closer cultures, the ideas of superiority and inferiority were, in their own often strange ways, prevalent. For example, the Ancient Greeks of Aristotle decided that their culture was superior not because of colour, but because theirs was based in the right climate for intelligent philosophical and existential thought and being (Aristotle, 2008). This idea, which understandably lost traction over a while, shows the immaturity of social constructions of difference. What it also displays is the fear of cultures residing close to one another that certain peoples have, and the lengths they will go to in order to distance themselves from the humanity of the cultural other.

The creation of race, out of the battles for certain cultures to have emergent superiority over others, followed the same route. The belittling of those cultures which were not seen as culturally civilised enough, be it in the arts or religion or any other fashion, has led to the marginalisation and denigration of huge groups of people over generations. That there is cultural destructiveness embedded within the construction of the racialised other should therefore not be underestimated. From the suppression of the languages of the Welsh to the suppression of the clothing of colonised Africans to the need to hide one's own Jewish name, cultural suppression is an aspect of the experience of racism (Jones, 1998; Mastroianni, 2015; Rovine & Rovine, 2018). To turn this around ninety degrees, I will add here that the soul-destroying dehumanisation which is race and racism is emergent out of the attempt of one culture to see itself as superior to all others under the grandiose gaze of systemic white supremacy.

The psychodynamics of racism

Yet, race is a construct, and it is here, so we need to understand its impact upon all of us. So, before we actually get into looking at the psychological and the traumatic impact of racism, we first of all have to lay out the ground of just how psychodynamic theory can help us understand what racism actually is. In order for us to do this, Figure 3.1, which highlights the psychodynamics of racism, looks at just how our socially constructed identities leave us to create an identity based around race and therefore racism.

Jean Piaget (Weil & Piaget, 1951) talked about how prejudice helps us all to form an aspect of our identity. His work, although built out of early ideas about social construction within psychotherapy, was taken that bit further by Francis Aboud (1993) who looked at how children navigate ideas of difference and diversity. To look at this through the ideas of race and racial formation, we also have to understand that the social constructions of white supremacy, patriarchy, and capitalism have a huge role in creating that part of our identity which is therefore prejudiced and, beyond that, racist towards other people and, I will argue here, towards ourselves.

Figure 3.1 speaks to this. First of all, we need to recognise that race and therefore racism on its own is a nothing. It does not actually exist. It is not a singular incident that happens in isolation. In order for it to matter, it has to happen in relationship with another group, another person, another entity, or another aspect of ourself. It

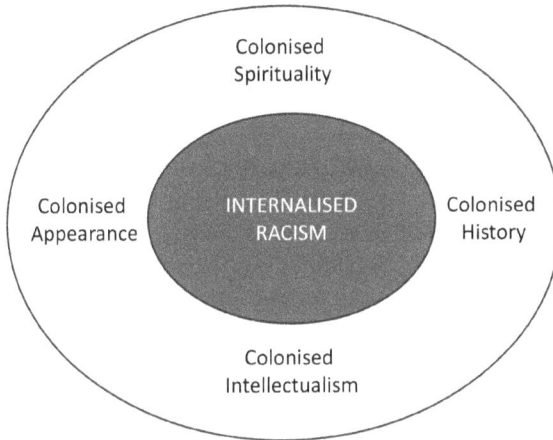

Figure 3.1 Personal impacts of racism

is important though to recognise that racism has drivers and it is these that actually move us to experience racism towards ourselves or to enact it upon another.

Envy is the first part of this. Envy is something which psychodynamic theorists, such as Melanie Klein (Mitchell, 1986) talk of as the desire to either possess something which is desirable in another person or, if one cannot have that, to destroy it. Envy is a core driver in racism. Yet, what I mean by this is that often, that which we hate through race or whatever else has something which we believe that we should have or that we should want. One of the more stereotypically driven, yet important to recognise, facets of antisemitism is that it is often underpinned by a level of the perceived power or wealth of said community; be it true or otherwise (Garcia-Navaro, 2023). Other ways that this could be seen is in the envy of those who wish to be darker skinned, for example, and how this envy is projected upon those who are persons of colour. This envy is then either enacted by wanting to destroy that which is the other, or to become that which is the other, using cosmetic means.

During the days of slavery, one of the things that was enacted most of all in the envious attacks upon the slaves who perhaps escaped or who were perhaps disobedient, was the emasculation of male slaves and the sexual abuses of women slaves (Akbar, 1984). The fear, and the envy of that which those who perceive themselves as holding the power of whiteness might have towards the culturalised other, was often the driving force towards said destruction of that which they could not have, own, or possess – for example their perceived superior sexuality.

With envy over-pinning racism, what we must also factor in is hate. Through a psychodynamic lens, hate is a force, I might argue here, which is driven by a fear that one cannot control or possess that which is hated (Alford, 2006; Frosh, 2005; N. Hall et al., 2014). Similar to a child who, because it cannot dominate the parent, at times has to hate said parent out of a fear of its own omnipotence being disrupted. Hate therefore becomes a massive factor regarding how we might manage the underlying fear of the other. Where racism actually comes in is that often times, when hate is enacted upon the cultural other, it is done so from a place of fear, a place of distress about the threats towards one's own systemic cultural identity.

An interesting example emerges out of the political scene in 2024. During March of that year, an issue with the Member of Parliament, Diane Abbott, stemmed from a Tory donor stating that, and I quote, 'It's like trying not to be racist, but you see Diane Abbott on TV and you just want to hate all black women because she's there and I don't hate all black women at all, but I think she should be shot' (Seddon & Crew, 2024). The level of vitriol within said statement about a Black, female MP raised such furore that it led to a call for this Tory donor's money to be given back to them by the Tory Party.

The interesting part about the statement, when seen through the lens of hate and how it is actually a core facet of racism, is that this man has obviously tied the two together, which is in its most simplistic form. Yet, in doing so, in stating that he is not racist and actually trying to underpin his idea that he has a right to say this, there is an underlying envy of Diane Abbott's position as a prominent woman of colour.

To emphasise this point, this level of misogynoir, or the hatred of Diane Abbot because she is an MP who holds a level of political power, that this power contrasts with an idea of specialness, of racialised specialism perhaps, that sits within a person who identifies as white in this instance, talks of the struggle which sits within ideas of race and racism (Bailey & Trudy, 2018). This struggle being that actually it is built around an idea of systemic white superiority. Constructs of identity, in particular the more biological ones, do not come with a natural sense of superior and inferior. Socially constructed aspects of identity do, and it is these which hold alongside themselves envy, hate, and I may argue here as well, fear, in order to bolster them and their position.

One cannot forget the other two of the horsemen of this systemic apocalypse, these being fear and shame because, as already intimated by the diagram, all four of these play roles in the maintenance and the systemic oppression of the other through racism. So, whereas envy and hate play obvious roles, fear also has a fairly obvious but sometimes quite subtle role in the maintenance and the subjugation of the racialised other. Fear in this instance could be anything from the fear of being marginalised to be seen as an outsider to, at its more extreme end, the fear of losing one's own life through some sort of racialised violence (King, 2015). The constant fear of other cultural groups, be they through the lens of antisemitism, Islamophobia, and other instances, is something which has often been used and manipulated by the political sphere as a means of controlling certain populations. That these are underpinned by the racism withheld within politics and also with the societies that politicians represent, should also not be underestimated (Stone, 2016; Tarr, 2015).

The politics of fear in its own way is the politics of racism, whereby fear of the other becomes the manipulation of internalised systemic racism towards said racialised other (King, 2015). The fear from a psychological perspective though, fear of the other, is also driven by a fear of the parts of ourselves which make us authentic (Hirose & Pih, 2011). Internally, when we talk about self-othering, it is not just that we have come to want to hate and distance ourselves from certain aspects of who we are, it is because we also internalised a fear of said aspects of our racialised identity. This internalisation being directed from outside of ourselves, via family, culture, gender, or some other part of our intersectional identity.

Self-hatred can come up in many forms and also holds within it a self-fear of our Blackness, of our Jewishness, of the fact that we are culturally separate and different, and can lead to us also finding ways to manipulate these parts of our identity in order to fit in. Code switching, colourism, racial passing are all ways in which the racialised other's fear of their own racial identity then leads them to marginalise that part of themselves, to want to kill it off or destroy it.

When we come to the issues of shame though, this is perhaps one of the more subtle ways in which racism self-perpetuates. Shaming the cultural other into compliance through a caricature of that other, is one of the most frequently used, but also one of the most deeply cutting, ways in which the subtlety of racism continues to find cultural purchase (Harrison, 2017). Shame of who it is to be a person of colour is something which would often be used by the media and by certain comedians for example, both in the United Kingdom and the United States, as a way of showing that there was one group that was culturally superior to another. The fact that so many of these age-old comedians are now calling out the woke majority for being overly touchy and sensitive, is actually just another way of dictating the narrative and shaming the other back into compliance (Harriot, 2022).

Another perhaps more obvious example of this comes up within the guise of stereotyping. When we stereotype, for example, Black women as being perhaps potentially angry at their treatment, what they are often left with is a sense that, should they speak up and stand up for what is often a perfectly reasonable request at some sort of change in individual of systemic behaviour, they will be shut down at best (Bailey & Trudy, 2018). The fear of doing so, the fear of being labelled, the fear of bringing shame upon oneself or onto one's community is what often leads to a silencing from that racialised position. Shame is used as a weapon to silence, much as fear is used as a weapon towards compliance and although I have separated out these four horsemen of the racialised apocalypse into different silos, they all interact within each other in varying ways.

Envy of the cultural other can often lead to a systemically moulded whiteness of the subject speaking up and out in crowded environments as a means of shaming the then racialised other into compliance (Johnson et al., 2021). Their underlying hatred of the fact that this person who they believe to be racially inferior to them is actually, if not an equal, also often a superior to who they happen to be, leads them to feel that they have to act out, to re-address this internalised systemic structure that they were born with and have imbibed.

Where there is a level of fear there is also the threat to the egoic structure around the race of the subject. What I mean by this is when said subject sees the other, the racialised other as an equal or not as subservient to them as they have been taught to be, there is a deep-seated and yet incredibly subtle sense of ego shattering that the subject then has to endure.

DiAngelo's (2018) work around white fragility, although rooted within an American structure of race, which is very binary, does very little to really explore the egoic fracturing that comes with seeing the racialised other outside of the stereotypical confines which have defined it within subjective spaces. The Black sports person who speaks up in a political sphere is therefore challenging the subjective, systemic racism that has defined them as being only a sports person and therefore not having a voice (Various, 2021).

The other interesting part of this whole discussion around the psychodynamics of race is that the external impact of this superior/inferior, master/slave dialectic as posited by Hegel (1976) and many other theorists, such as Fanon (2005) is that this also forms a part of the internal world as well. When we look at this superior/inferior racialised dynamic and we place it within an internal context, then what we often have to understand is that experiences of racism lead to a level of splitting between that which is seen as desirable from within the context of superiority versus those aspects which have been racially denoted to be seen as the other, and therefore as less desirable by the societal construct we all reside within.

We may make jokes about the physical features of a person of colour, of a person who is Jewish, or a person who is from a travelling community, or South Asian, and those jokes may well be built around ideas of racialised superiority, as they would have been on television screens back in the 1970s and 1980s. Those internalisations of said jokes, comments, and statements, through the repeated influence of these, can then also lead to persons on the receiving end, who identify as the racialised other, wanting to distance themselves from those characteristics, those ways of being, those behaviours, which mark themselves out as separate, as distinctly different (S. Hall, 1996).

This brings in the idea of splitting; when we often talk about splitting, what we will have to start to recognise is that splitting has an element within it of being provoked by the socially constructed aspects of identity that we all hold. Psychodynamic splitting, as posed by Klein (Mitchell, 1986) is often seen in a relationship between self and another, normally the mother or a parent or caregiver. What we need to recognise is that psychological splitting is also a facet of the construction of the racialised identity of the racialised other. The fear of that splitting though, is often what drives certain communities to hold themselves together, and this drive for unity, cultural or racialised, is often, in its over-exaggeration and sometimes stereotypical nature, through rituals and the adherence to cultural norms; a response and reaction to the externalised cultures which sit outside of oneself, and which want to either consciously or unconsciously disrupt the racialised structures within one's own cultural environment.

Fear, again, plays a role in this, and this is why, for example across the Global North, the rise of populism has been so prevalent within the political arena (Kaltwasser Rovira et al., 2019). That fear of the migrant other, the immigrant other, the cultural other, whilst one could consider to be authentic and genuine, is also something which can be manipulated and co-opted by political parties in their attempts to either obtain or maintain power. The drive to profit from the fear of cultural dilution is also something which sits within the incredible conspiracy theory called 'the great replacement' (Burns, 2023; Goetz, 2021). To say a small amount about this, this is the idea often posited from within a white supremacist framework, that cultures, groups, migrants, are working together to actually replace those who identify as white via their colour and their race, to therefore wipe them out.

Ideas such as this then drive the external and internal splits of those who are on the racialised receiving end of the power and therefore the trauma used to maintain the cultural structure of the supremacist. For those who are on the receiving end, however, much of this fear, much of the envy, much of the hatred that they have to endure within the framework of understanding racism of course has deeper psychological and traumatic impacts.

The developmental stages of racism

Previously, in the story of Reggie, the fact that he was raised as the only person of colour in his community meant that, as an adult in our work, he had numerous experiences of what we would now term as micro-aggressions but which actually, over a period of time, he realised had cut him really deeply. He offered me one example: when he was about seven or eight, he had tackled a boy in his school whilst they were playing football; the boy, who was the same age as him, then got up, called him the "N" word, and ran off to continue the game. Reggie complained to a teacher about this experience and the teacher just shrugged and said he would just have to get on with it and there was nothing he could do, leaving the him bereft and alone with his experience. Moreover, on reporting this to his mother, who was white Scandinavian, she herself did not know how to approach this and did nothing herself to either help or support her son.

When being told this story, not only was it heartbreaking for me to hear, and not only was this a reminder of some of my own earliest experiences, but what it also gave me in the present era was an insight into just how alienating and alienated a good number of persons of racialised difference are from the very earliest of ages.

Racism has a developmental edge. Therefore, to explore the developmental stages around this, I have constructed my own table, Figure 3.2, which is modelled upon Frances Aboud alongside one or two ideas of Du Bois and my own theories as to the developmental states that children go through when they have to construct their racialised identity and experience of racism (Aboud, 1993; Du Bois, 1903).

Figure 3.2 explores this in detail. To say a bit more though, between the ages of zero and two, when a child is very much a baby, there is this very interesting visualisation of a baby as just a baby (meaning they are non-racialised). Even if they are of a different culture, of a distinct colour, because they are a baby and because they are also fairly helpless, the odds are that they are not going to be seen as any type of threat to the systemic whiteness of those around them, be they from within their culture or without.

It is hugely important to continue to recognise this and for those who are seen as the racialised other. It often means that this may be one of the few times when the

The Development of the Socially Constructed Racial Identity		
0-2	The parents may well enact double consciousness, meaning they will perform authentically in the home, whilst adaptively outside of home.	• The period where the baby is least racialised. • Within the home, the racialisation of the baby is at a minimum, unless there is racial trauma within the family system. • The child is mostly offered the privilege of being seen as a child outside of the home.
3-6	The parents begin to mould the child to the structures of white supremacy, so as to make the child appear safe. The parent hides from the oppressiveness of their own experiences as a racialised other, thereby (unconsciously) abandoning the child to their own racial experiences.	• Society increasingly sees the child as a racialised object, and therefore begins to see them with fear or hatred. • The child is increasingly problematised when they do not conform to the racial stereotypes society places upon them. • The internalisation of this experience leads to internalised splitting of the self along racial lines, childhood is lost, and the adultification of the child begins.
7-8	Or, the parents begin to fight on behalf of the child in racialised situations and environments.	• The privilege of childhood no longer exists for the racialised child, as they are fully experienced via their societal racial identity. • This adultification of the child becomes deeply embedded within the racialised self. • The child may adapt to survive or be marked out by society as problematic. • The double consciousness, or the splitting of the authentic racial self into the shadow, continues here apace.

Figure 3.2 Developmental stages of racial identity formation

baby is allowed the privilege, and I am using that word for a reason, to be seen in all their innocence. One of the tricky things about growing up as a child in environments in which race and racism are going to be prevalent, is that one has to give up one's youthfulness and innocence fairly quickly to learn to adapt to the systemic messages passed onto and through us. The adultification of children therefore has a racialised component within it (Cooke & Halberstadt, 2021).

The other part to mention here is that between the ages of zero and two children, according to Aboud (1988, 1993) really recognise what is them and what is not them. They start to mimic the behaviour of adults. This then raises an interesting conundrum. If the parents are themselves colonised to be a certain way, to perform their racialised identity in a way that is seen as non-offensive and non-threatening by those imbued with whiteness, then these adaptations are going to start to occur from the moment the child is born. Du Bois' ideas of double consciousness sit here, his view being centred around the fact that actually persons of colour will early on, and at a stage of preverbal development, begin to have a double sense of who they are – that this will involve a forward-facing persona type safety, versus a more authentic racialised sense of who they are behind closed doors (Cullen Rath, 1997; Du Bois, 1903).

Making sense of this for the racialised child therefore will be difficult because there are pre-verbal messages which are passed on to the child unconsciously by the actions of those around them and of the society around them. The pleasure of being an innocent one versus the recognition that actually not all is as it seems. The double consciousness, therefore, is something which, because it occurs so early and so pre-verbally, can probably be best explored within counselling and psychotherapy by using techniques that engage with the preverbal unconscious. This therefore means that creative techniques such as sand play, dreamwork, visualisations, the work of Internal Family Systems, for example, are all beneficial ways to explore the unconscious landscape of the burgeoning child as they form a racialised sense of who they are (X. Hunt & Swartz, 2017; E. R. Taylor, 2009). These adaptations will appear in the very annals and depths of the pre-egoic shadow.

The importance of recognising that double consciousness, performativity, and code switching are taught to a child of racial difference from almost its inception, should not be underestimated. The impact of witnessing one's own parents and caregivers switch and change their behaviours in certain environments is something which, within this theory and based upon my experience, means that the impact of racism is a keenly and instantaneously felt one.

Mimicry or mimesis also fits into this arena (Bell, 1999; Ram, 2014). The ability to mimic the behaviour of others around us is something which sits within many unfamiliar cultures and forms the bedrock for much of how we interact with the world, how we view the world, and also our ability to witness the creative within our worlds. Watching actors upon a stage, we often do not just imagine said actor playing the role of Othello, of Malcolm X, of Wonder Woman, or of any other character, thereby taking them out of the original life, but we can also imagine ourselves playing said role of Martin Luther King, of Queen Elizabeth II, or of Agatha Christie. We want to be those roles because we want to mimic the ideas presented before us on said screen, in a book, a picture, an image or a narrative of some other type.

For Aboud, between the ages of three and six is where a child starts to work out what is them, and what is not them. Although they are unable to empathise with the other, what Aboud suggests is that they are able to start to separate out and recognise their own grouping and their own type of separateness from those around them. Having already talked about mimicry, this adaptation, this ability that Aboud speaks of to play the roles of the other and recognise their own separateness from the other, then brings into play the ability to move between certain worlds. The ways that children of racialised difference will perform in order to fit in, will put on a certain voice, will act a certain way, is something which children are often taught as they recognise that in order for them to be accepted, they have to play out a certain role, a certain way of being.

In my own life, the idea that when we went to church at five years of age, we would have to dress in our Sunday finest, with good shoes, good trousers, a jacket, a shirt and a tie, and we would have to stand in patient rows, slightly behind and alongside our mother, in order to present a pleasant face for Father 'Whoever' after he gave his sermon that day, is a way of showing how well we had to perform in order to fit into a religious, white, colonised narrative. There were also times though, where if we did not behave within that colonial framework, we were told in no uncertain terms that our behaviour had brought shame upon our mother and that it should not happen again.

Now this is not so much to give one's own parents a challenging time because they themselves would have endured similar behaviour, but it is to emphasise the fact that these lessons are quite powerful as they come in from outside. Other examples of this also involve the overt and often covert lessons passed from parents to children of racialised difference, to encourage them to behave in a certain way whilst engaging in their day-to-day school life.

The racialised impact of nursery which starts between the ages of three and six should also be factored in. The lessons that are taught of reading and writing are not the only ones that a child of racialised difference imbibes. There are also cultural lessons about performance, about behaviour, about actions and about ways of being which, if not internalised 'correctly' by the child can then lead to that child of racialised difference to be seen as a problem in some ways, or in more severe ways to be seen as psychologically unwell and therefore unable to be seen within said school environment. The number of children who struggle in that space between home and school, where they are challenged with finding a different identity would be reflected in the exclusion rates for certain groups; for example, the Gypsy and Roma, and traveller of Irish heritage pupils had the highest permanent exclusion rates in the 2021 to 2022 school year – both had 31 exclusions for every 10,000 pupils (or 0.31%) (Various, 2024, p. 1).

The idea that children from a racialised background have therefore to conform to a distinct cultural narrative, a racialised one, which not only marginalises those of the racialised other, but also inhibits the performance and the abilities of different genders, people from different class, is something which I have discussed in the previous chapters – an adaptation which has resided within the educational establishment, in the United Kingdom, and also other countries across the Global North since the days of colonialism. Often the rebelliousness that we see within certain children as they try and stand up for themselves is actually not much more than an anger at their own inauthenticity, the struggle to individuate and to be one's own self, a fire which can be dampened and eventually put out within education. The struggles for Reggie, my client from earlier on, to fit in within this paradigm also held an influence for my client Sylvia, whose story I will tell below.

Sylvia was a 38-year-old woman who I worked with. A woman with a Romany background, her mother left said environment when she met and married an Englishman when Sylvia was no more than two years of age. On coming to the United Kingdom though, Sylvia struggled to fit in. On her first experiences of nursery and school, Sylvia noticed several things.

The first was that the other mothers at the school would often shun Sylvia's mother because she was considered quite an attractive woman; these other mothers saw her as a threat to them and to their own marriages. This therefore meant that Sylvia witnessed the sadness and isolation of her own mother because she was different. The second aspect was that she had very few friends in her nursery and into the early years of primary school. Other children would turn their backs on her because she was quite obviously not like them, they would turn their backs on her in the playground when she asked if she could play with them, and there were even occasions where some of the other children called her dirty, pulled her hair, and hit her. None of these incidents, even if they were noticed by the teachers, were ever challenged, meaning that often-times Sylvia was quite readily left on her own to cope with these experiences of marginalisation and racism based upon her cultural background.

Our work together though, was not so much about therapy because Sylvia had found a way forward through her life, whereby she felt able to establish herself in her career, standing up for the marginalised and in particular those children from immigrant backgrounds who themselves found it difficult to find a place within this culture. The one area where she did struggle, she acknowledged, was in the formation of trusting relationships, and in her mid-thirties Sylvia, who was from the LGBTQ community had still not felt herself ready to find a partner with whom she felt safe enough to establish a deep and trusting relationship.

This example in some ways hints at some of the psychological damage which children who have been marginalised because of their racial difference then carry forward into their adult lives. It needs to be noted though that this marginalisation, this fear of being one's own self, this trauma of having one's own identity which one cannot change, which is denigrated and hated, is something which can become internalised like any other experience.

The ages of seven onwards are important. As stated, that anger at one's own racial inauthenticity starts at quite an early age for most children. My experience around working with and being around children of racial difference is that this anger, this fire starts to build from that age onwards. The anger at having to split and play a role of performativity which, as I have already explored, starts quite early on.

The reasons for this touches on some of Aboud's (1993) other ideas about this time in a child's life. Aboud explored the idea that children feel a sense of shame or pride about their racialised identity at about this age. My experience dictates that that sense of shame, that sense of pride, that sense of anger, that sense of happiness, if it is allowed, can be quite a healing process. In the modern era, for example, we have a lot of schools who carry out things like Black History Month or explore what it is to be from a Muslim background, the idols from different racial groupings, thereby allowing certain children to feel a certain level of connective pride and authenticity about who they happen to be.

When this does not happen and when there is not the space for the feelings that I have just described, then my experience is that what happens for children of racialised difference is that these feelings either get acted out and played out within the wider familial, schooling, or societal environment, or they become internalised and repressed. That sense of shame that some children of a certain age would have felt when watching Roots back in the 1970s and 1980s (Beresford et al., 2016). Or, that sense of shame experienced by other racialised groupings who have since been labelled as flawed, as terrorists, as something to be hated and feared, can often find itself hidden away through performativity in its most basic element, but also through the hiding away of who one actually truly is, a rejection of those racialised identities via code switching, name changing, and other means that one might employ.

There is a children's book named *Sulwe* (Lupita, 2021) which speaks to the problems children can encounter when forming their racial identity. This book tells the story of a young, Black girl, of around 7 years of age, who because she is darker skinned than her sister, finds herself marginalised by her sister's friends. She also wishes to be like her, to have lighter skin so she could fit in with her peers. She starts to self-hate her own identity by not only trying to scrub her dark skin white but trying to eat the whitest of foods she can possibly find to change her racialised identity. Of course, none of this actually works and eventually she finds a way of accepting her racialised sense of self and noticing the fact that she is beautiful as she is. The reason for me telling this story so briefly in this chapter is to express how hard it is for children of racialised difference, even within colonised countries to come to terms with the internalised coloniser, which has been taken on board from such an early and young stage of development.

One of the other aspects to consider when we look at the developmental stages that children go through when encountering racism, be it at home, with their caregivers, in society or at school, is that there is a gradual, cultural erasure that happens for said child. This does not happen for all children. There are some cultures whereby although they experience a great deal of racism, the cultural framework is strong enough and firm enough to semi-withstand some of the hate and prejudice raised against it. The bonding together of certain groups, be they South Asian, Jewish, Romany or from other communities, therefore becomes a semi-antidote to some of this material.

When using the word 'semi', what I actually mean is that it is impossible to fully avoid the impact of systemic racism upon one's community and therefore on oneself, in particular as a child. Ways in which one may avoid said impacts are things we have already discussed such as performativity or code switching, but there is also another one – echoism.

Echoism, which is something that is emergent from the original Greek myth of Narcissus, then becomes a form of performance in its own right (Ovid, 2015). In this instance though, it becomes a way in which one mirrors back to the collective, to those who hold systemic power, that which is special within themselves whilst denigrating one's own self into the process (Davis, 2005; Shirock, 2013). Echoism, like performativity, like code switching, also leaves the other, aka the racialised other, unseen, unwitnessed, and incomplete. This is the nature of the echo. In many ways it is insubstantial in its own self and the ability to be fully oneself, to be authentic within one's own right, then becomes the privilege and the domain of those who hold systemic and narcissistic power.

The erasure of one's authentic cultural identity, one's cultural self and other aspects, aids the process of the creation and 'echoising' of the racialised other. What this also does is it reinforces the internalisation that it is unsafe to be one's own self. The double consciousness that I have already spoken about, the ability to adapt to systemic white spaces as discussed in the works of Angelou (1984) are things which then become the domain of all who are on the receiving end of these racialised aspects.

Given that race is not a construct built from colour, even those who may see themselves as white skinned will still perform in some way or fashion a form of racialised whiteness as ascribed to them. Celts, for example, those who may reject their own sort of cultural heritage in order to fit in with a white English idea of what it is to be white, perform and play into this idea of echoistic representation and the uplifting of white supremacy. Our idea of whiteness is also challenged in these aspects, which is another part of this psychological exploration. The idea that there is one way of being white is what drives so many of us through said internalisations to perform whiteness, as opposed to recognising that racial identity is not centred around a colour, a form of whiteness. This is something which, when we work through it, we get to regain and reclaim for our own self, should we wish to do so. I will discuss this further in Chapter 5

Identity, as it has been co-opted by the systemic centre, then has a great deal to answer for in the corruption of the early innocence of so many. The repressive triumvirate which has become internalised in its constant messaging of inadequacy down to the racialised other, then manipulates said racialised aspects of the identity of the other into compliance and conformity. There is an implanting at this same stage of a sense of shame; nay not so much an implanting but an invigorating of said shame so that it becomes something to be avoided and something that we must try and reject at all costs. These social constructions or identity, and I am saying this through the lens of race in this instance, worked very much upon the idea that whatever is passed through us through society's expectations of how we are supposed to be, thereby uses shame to mould us into conformity.

Even the politics of our times has spoken to this. The idea that when immigrants moved to the Global North they should conform to colonised ways of being, is something which sits very central to the political narratives of integration (Ciaian & Kancs, 2019; Oliver-Dee, 2017). The failure therefore of these processes to recognise that movements of immigrants will inevitably bring not only benefits, but also cultural and system change by their very nature; and the failure to accept this as normal, as a part of the process of culture, is part of the reason why there is such a struggle to move back to ways before, to hark back to the past, to idolise historical times where things were that bit purer and more innocent – to become more embedded within a racially narcissistic fantasy.

Moving back to the impact upon children, another area to consider is how underplayed and under-recognised these aspects of racism are upon children. I have given you several stories already in this text which talk about the individual experiences of racism, and I have quoted statistics which have looked at how these experiences have been met across whole groupings. However, when we factor in something such as the Adverse Childhood Experience (ACE) framework, then what we start to see is that a framework that is designed to look at the difficult experiences of childhood leaves a massive hole when it comes to considerations of racism.

To say a little bit more about the ACE framework, this was a framework designed by Vincent Felitti, through the Centre for Disease Control and Prevention, between 1995 and 1997 (RMCH, 2022). This framework has expanded gradually over time to include ten different areas; it emphasises that these are particular ways and experiences for children which may lead them to suffer from psychological harm and damage. These could be anything from domestic abuse to adverse mental illness within the home.

This is a framework which has been adapted and adopted by numerous countries across the Global North and is something which has often underpinned the childhood services of said nations; however, whilst it does some decent work in many different ways, it has its flaws. The Welsh Government, in a report published fairly recently, in one of its criticisms of the ACE framework recognised that the absence of socio-economic and cultural experience for children was a huge flaw in the exploration and recognition that children experienced more difficulties than just those currently laid out through ACE (J. Taylor & Welsh Government, 2021).

I am going to add to the statements made through the Welsh Government when I state that, given how prevalent racism is for vast numbers of children, to reject and ignore this experience falls into the systemic idea that racism does not exist within white society. Coupling this with the idea, also raised as a criticism of ACE, that some of this framework is very much built upon the ideas of white supremacy and that it has not been explored through different cultural lenses, there is a danger as well that a framework such as this has found itself very much embedded within the supremacy and the structures of inequality and hatred that it also attempts to disrupt.

A framework such as ACE, which has a lot to offer I might add, is ultimately, I believe, a framework that is constantly evolving and should over time incorporate the ways in which race and racism and how we cope with these aspects as minority groups impact upon the neurological, psychological, physiological, and trauma experiences of children accordingly.

The neurological impact of racism

In 1997, in a report commissioned by the Human Rights and Equal Opportunities Commission of Australia entitled Bringing Them Home, close consideration was given to the impact on former Aboriginal children of a policy which the Australian government advocated for when they were separated from their families at an early age (Human Rights and Equal Opportunity Commission, 1997). This report considered the background to this policy, how it was very much rooted in the racism of the time and within ideas which involved attempts to *civilise* Aboriginal children by placing them with white, coloniser families. A policy which has since been called a form of genocide, this policy ran for decades and led to the forced removal and the separation of children from their families of origin.

However, one of the core parts of this report, as written by the Commission of Australia, was their recognition of the psychological and neurological impacts of the reversal of this process and the mental health impact of it ending so suddenly, an impact which left so many traumatised by said separation. The report goes into great detail regarding the increased levels of alcohol abuse, drug abuse, and ongoing mental health conditions from the systemic racism they endured. As explored in the report as well, although oftentimes these children were placed with white families, with the driving force to be to civilise them into colonial societies, what often happened with these children was they were still ostracised within said families because they were seen as outsiders, therefore enduring a secondary level of racism because of said separation.

Given the stages that I have spoken about in the previous sections of this chapter, it is worth noting the importance of this extra layer. These were children who would have formed familial and community bonds with their caregivers and were then not only moved from within that community system, but were then placed within a more binary, hierarchical system alien to themselves. The psychological and neurological shock of such incidents must have been enormous for some of those children, let alone for the parents and communities who gave birth to said children.

It is important to look at the differing ways in which racism impacts upon the whole sense of self of those on the receiving end of said experiences. The difficulty in writing these different sections to this book, though, is that there can be a preponderance or an attempt to see these as hierarchical. Figure 3.3 shows how all of these aspects, early life development, neurological, health impacts, and trauma

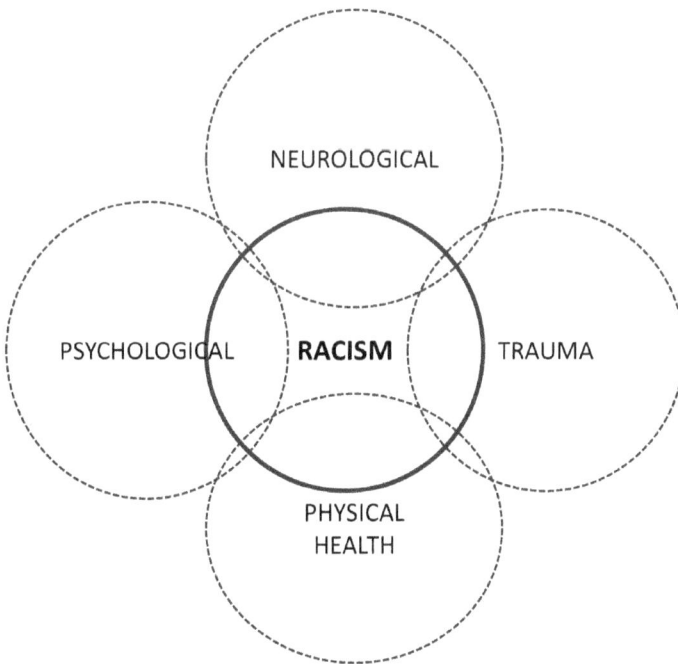

Figure 3.3 Psychological impacts of racism

impacts, are actually a bit like the parts of a clock. They sit together, interplaying with each other at all times, so although I am going to talk in this particular section about the neurological impact of racism, it is in no way separate from that of trauma, no way detached from the early life experience of racism, and no way separate from the physical health impacts of racism.

To say more about this, there was an interesting report out of the Centre for Disease Control in the United States, which was summarised in the *Mail Online* in 2023, and undertook an exploration of the neurological impact of racism (Joshu, 2023). A research project that explored one hundred people's experiences of discrimination and the participants then underwent MRI scans as part of the research, which revealed some interesting results. The research also involved the showing of said participants' pictures of unhealthy foods, foods that were more sugar and fat filled. The research recognised that people who were exposed to discrimination would be more often predisposed to crave unhealthy foods, with the research actually going a bit deeper and recognising that this craving was in some way to mitigate against the unhealthy feelings and experiences of racism. The impact neurologically of this also recognised within this research that there had been an increased preponderance towards obesity and other health-related conditions based around the internalised neurological impact of racism.

Following on from the reports that I have actually outlined here, which speak to experiences of racism across the world, what we start to see is that the experiences of racialised displacement, of racialised hatred, and of racialised adaptation and double consciousness, then inevitably have links to the neurological distress of a large number of racialised peoples. The fact that neuroscience is now beginning to track the impact of oppression and the continued impact neurologically of racism, actually in some ways counters some of the more minimising narratives that sit within the worlds of psychology, counselling, and psychotherapy.

What I mean by this is when we look at things such as microaggressions, the term alone lends itself to a pseudo-understanding of racism as being something which is small in nature and therefore has less of an impact. When we factor in neuroscience and the traumatic impact of racism, what we start to see, though, is that ways for those on the receiving end of dealing with the constant, multiple slings, and arrows of racist incidents, micro though they might be, in their regularity and in their intensity, often lead to individuals having to form coping mechanisms in order to deal with the neurological, psychological, and traumatic impacts of racism.

To expand on this a little bit further, if we begin to see racism as a form of trauma, and if we begin to recognise that trauma has a neurological facet, then ways of working within counselling and psychotherapy, such as EMDR (Eye Movement Desensitisation and Reprocessing), lend themselves to a more inclusive way of working with these difficult experiences (Various, 2023). EMDR by its very nature recognises that trauma gets stuck in one part of the brain; a system of interviews and ways of working which sets up safe spaces within the neurological framework, then allows clients to build neurological pathways between various parts of the brain so that experiences of trauma can be processed.

The health impact of racism

In a paper on daynurseries.co.uk of racialised children in nursery care in the United Kingdom, some shocking issues were raised (Albert, 2021). Within this study, there was a recognition that, more often than not, children of colour or racialised difference, whilst in nursery and within certain childcare institutions and environments, were less likely to be held, cuddled, or changed by those in whose care they had been entrusted. This would often lead to distress, not only for the parents, but for their children as well.

The psychological impact of the racism of those types of caregivers not only has its roots in a capitalist system which sees childcare as a business and not as a right for those who have been charged with upkeeping said system, but also does not recognise the subtle layers of anti-other racism which will probably have been internalised by said caregivers, even before they receive any children. That there is little to no addressing of what I call people's embodiments within systems of racism is a huge flaw in the caregiving system and understandably would have led to the mistreatment and mis-care of a sizeable number of children.

The example that I gave you in the previous chapter, of the client who struggled at his school over a number of years, holds parallels but also differences to the experience that I endured whilst I was a child. Whereas for the client, there was no respite from his experience at secondary school, where there were no teachers whom he could rely on or who would stand up for him, and where he was very much left on his own to get over his experiences and get on with just living life, in my primary school, I was fortunate to have primary school Head Teachers who were a bit more forward thinking about race and racism and stood up for me in ways that I could not have foreseen.

The sadness and shame that the client felt at his own Blackness and his own racialised otherness, meant that he tried overly hard to fit into white Scandinavian society. The alcoholism, the drug use, and the other health issues that I have already briefly touched on in this chapter, are facets of the ongoing struggle that those who are racially different, and who have been marked as such, encounter and internalise in their experiences.

The health impacts of racism are many, with the links between racism, neurological impacts, trauma, and increased levels of obesity, diabetes, and other health concerns, are an ongoing area of understanding which is gradually being eked out in current discourse and research. From the United Nations to British services, varying research projects have been put in place to explore this growing area, and what is becoming increasingly apparent is that we have under-estimated the psychological weight that those who are racially the other have to carry, both psychologically, literally, and symbolically when they encounter experiences of racism.

When we consider the health implications of racism, it is important to take a deeper dive into some of the literature that links race and racism to physical disorders. Edward Tull and his team at the University of the Caribbean, in a series of papers which were researched looked at just how racist incidents were a contributing factor to increased levels of obesity for persons of difference (Butler et al., 2002; Tull et al., 1999). Their studies looked at how obesity and other physical ailments were connected to increased experiences of racism, drawing a distinct line between the psychological and the physical. In further research which has been corroborated by other universities, both in the United States and the UK there were subsequent links drawn between racism and other health issues, such as alcohol abuse (Drazdowski et al., 2016). A story passed to myself by a client, whose relatives were from the north of Sri Lanka, then brought this to my attention in a way that I had not expected.

> The client, who I will just give the initial S for this example, talked to me about his family's experience in coming from Northern Sri Lanka to the United Kingdom when he was a child. For those of you who are unaware, there had been a war in Sri Lanka for a number of years between those in the north and people in the south between 2008 and 2009. This led to a number of refugees from the north coming to the UK seeking a safe space to reside whilst the war continued, in the hope that it would end swiftly. S and his family were one of these groups to come to the United Kingdom, ending up in northwest London.

> S's father was a well-qualified man back in his homeland, yet when he came to the UK he was told that his qualifications did not compare, did not translate, and that he would need to either re-train, which would have cost several thousands of pounds, or he would need to take a less qualified position as a first starting point in the UK.

> In our work together, S and I looked at the systemic and institutional racism and prejudice which underpins these ideas. The idea being that if one is from the Global North and one trains here, that one's qualifications are therefore significantly better than those from Sri Lanka and other parts of the world. This is particularly important, especially given the fact that many of these training courses were established during colonial times and would have had a very much Eurocentric focus and basis to their structures and their learnings.

> The second part for S was the institutional racism that he endured whilst both applying for and actually undertaking jobs in this country. S's father worked as a maintenance person within a hospital for a company contracted to undertake such work. The struggle for S was that even though he was well qualified, and even though he was well respected by some of his colleagues and those where he was working, his boss made sure that he got the more difficult shifts, according to S, which if he refused would lead to subsequent punishments include anything from the removal of shifts to verbal put downs in front of his colleagues. His father, in order to cope, took up drinking. For S this was particularly traumatic because, back in their homeland, S had never

seen his father drink at all. This led to a breakdown of a psychological nature as well as physical ailments, so the family had to rally around and support S's father.

My work with S, though, was as much about what it was like for him to witness his father going through such difficult experiences, as it was to assist S himself in managing the transition from his homeland to a country which, in S's own words, was 'horribly racist' in a way that he had never foreseen.

This brief example talks about the health and psychological influences and, more so, the impacts of racism upon the racialised other. In this particular case, with S's father, the impact also rippled out to the wider family, so much so that they all ended up struggling with the impact of individual, institutional, and systemic racism which denigrated and minimised the life experience, the humanity of an individual who had already endured a difficult separation because of a war.

The trauma of racism

An obvious segue within this exploration then has to link racism and trauma. For those who have undergone some sort of experience of racism, the trauma of said experience is something which is very difficult to put a finger on, but it is important to do so as well. In a recent report out of the United States, studies have been conducted upon the link between racism and post-traumatic stress disorder, recognising that actually these experiences of racism have a deeper psychological impact and that they are really quite traumatic to both experience and also to witness.

My own self-care, for example, is often built around the idea that if something massively traumatic around race happens out in the world, I will think long and hard about whether I want to engage with it in the social media spheres of Twitter (not called X), LinkedIn, Instagram, and so on. Or if I want to ration that, knowing that this may well have an impact upon my mental health.

Vicarious trauma (Devilly et al., 2009; Sabin-Farrell & Turpin, 2003), which is an area that is often considered by therapists when working with and hearing experiences that are particularly troubling and traumatic, is another lens by which we can explore this. For most psychotherapists and counsellors, their use of personal therapy and supervision then becomes a way by which they can divest themselves of the fuller internalisations of the traumas of what we are witnessing and hearing. Given that racism also has a neurological, psychological, and physical impact, and that the vast majority of the racialised others will not be counsellors and psychotherapists, we then underestimate the layers of initial and secondary trauma which so many people endure. The physical and the psychological collide here with symptoms often appearing as they would in some other forms of trauma. These will include things like alcoholism and substances misuse, which I have already discussed, sleep disturbances, over-eating to compensate, and may also include ways of divesting oneself of said experiences by lashing out against others around.

I will suggest here that if we are going to look at the psychological and traumatic impacts of racism, it is important for future researchers to consider the possible connection between racism and things such as domestic abuse. This is not to excuse any abuser in the home, but it is to raise an amber to red flag around the intersecting layers of societal abuse that people may have endured, the impact and rage of which has nowhere to go and is then expressed within the home by either party.

The next thing to look at when we consider the link between trauma and racism, is actually the links between racism and suicide. A number of studies have come out both through the United Nations and across the world which have done an impressive job of linking bullying and suicide, be it in schools or as a form of cyberbullying (I. M. Hunt et al., 2021; Rockett et al., 2006; Zerach, 2016). Although online spaces are given over to the expression of many, many rich and wonderful experiences, how much of this space has also become a play park for the display of some of the worst amounts of previously contained hatreds that reside within so many of us should also be considered. Racism is one of these and the racialised hatred towards other people in that uncontained, non-super egoic sort of environment then has a psychological and often devastating impact on those on the receiving end.

I myself, at the age of 14, when attending a secondary school, was told I was very much the outsider, and experienced varying levels of interpersonal racism from my peers, as well as institutional systemic racism by the school. It was no surprise that I considered taking my own life at the age of 15 because there was nowhere for me to go and no space for me to explore these difficult experiences. Now, my own experience is just the experience of one person, so I place this story here as a means of helping others to understand that these internalisations and these deaths by a thousand cuts of racism, and what we term microaggressions, often lead to deeper psychological malaise, more so than we actually realise in many ways.

In their own research, which I think holds a lot of merit, the Samaritans importantly add an extra layer in their work because theirs is an organisation, perhaps one of those sorts of final spaces, for those who have felt that they do not have any other space to talk about their experiences. Here people can go and safely, and often anonymously, explore the impact of racism – the fact there is often no other space to go and speak about the racism they have endured, and the pain which they are still holding (Samaritans, 2014, 2021).

Working psychologically with the trauma of racism

When considering how racism impacts upon the psychological, the physical, and its link to trauma, practitioners therefore need to be a lot more aware of the connection between the external, wider, societal world and the internalisations which clients often unconsciously walk into the psychological, therapeutic space holding.

When we return to the example of S, our work therefore involved looking at the impact upon him of his father's drinking and also on the direct impact upon S of the racism that he himself endured whilst at school. This area was what actually brought him into therapy in the first instance. S had been picked on by his peers in a school in London from secondary age, firstly because he found it difficult to speak the English language but also because he was immediately marked as an outsider both by persons who would identify as racially white and as those who would identify as racially Black and South Asian. These levels of marginalisation led S to feel increasingly isolated. Together with the sense that there was no respite from these experiences of racialised otherness, be it at home and at school, S found himself falling into a depression and at times was tempted to misuse drugs and alcohol as he grew older. Fortunately for S, he found himself a fairly decent job after university where he just about passed his degree. The problems, though, had come to a head for S because his father had fallen ill, thereby raising the spectre of all that they had endured since arriving in the United Kingdom.

Our work was therefore to give S space to talk about the societal impact of racism, the economic ones, the racism of his peers, and the impact upon his family which he himself had internalised. We spent a lot of time utilising many different modalities when approaching S's world, having to adapt those modalities in order to meet the cultural constructs within S's internal family system or, in other words, his internalised sub-personalities. Working creatively with S helped most of all. Using sand play work, visualisation work and meditation in particular, actually reconnected S with aspects of his cultural heritage, which he had been encouraged to put aside in order to fit into a more English way of life.

The work with S was not necessarily one of total success but it did allow S to begin walking a path whereby he felt better able to be more himself and more able to deal with the internalisations of the impact of racism which were beginning to be passed down a generation from his father's experience.

Working with the trauma, the psychological, and the neurological impact of racism therefore allows us to explore in a more complete and complex fashion the deeper experiences of racism that so many of us have internalised. When we just see racism as something that we cannot approach or which we are too afraid to address in the psychotherapeutic space, what we end up doing is avoiding or ignoring the deep psychological wounding that so many racialised others encounter in majority environments. This avoidance in a way becomes an ethical issue because in some ways we are not quite doing the work that we have chosen to do, which is to help alleviate the pain and the stress of existence. So, given that racism, a part of the racial construct, is therefore also a part of our lived experience as human beings which we shy away from even approaching, is a bit like seeing an open doorway to a better world and choosing not to walk through it because we are just plainly too afraid.

Personal reflections on the internalisation of racism

Returning to the example that opened this chapter, in researching this book and looking not just at the experiences of racism that people endure in and around the world, but also at my own experiences of racism growing up, this research has helped me to make some of the following connections, or even to reconnect parts of myself that I had not realised were at play.

When I was 14 years of age, I had endured the caning by my principal for something which was not really my fault and for an incident which perhaps today would have led to that other student being suspended from the school. Yet, back then, because there was no what I considered justice, any sort of anger and upset that I had at being caned had to be held within myself and repressed. That was the summer that I realised I very much did not want to get up and do anything at all. I would stay in bed most days, sleeping long hours until the middle of the afternoon, and whilst many a parent reading this might say, 'Well, that's fairly normal for a boy', adding in the layers of lack of self-care, the fact that I would barely wash or clean myself for days or brush my teeth brings to light the fact that actually what I was going through in such a schooling environment was not only incredibly difficult but also incredibly isolating, lonely, and taken out on my own physical self.

Looking back there is a line that I can trace through having to endure the racist bullying of school days to a part of myself which, come the age of 15, actually wanted nothing more than to end my own life and leave this mortal coil. I had made plans to end my days but chose not to actually do so in the end because I started to write a diary. I wrote a lot about what it was like for me to be me; the things that I would do, the things I would not do, the sadness that I felt, and it was only through this reflexivity that I was able to discover the deeper parts of myself and explore those parts of myself which, years later, would form the bedrock of who I am from a racialised perspective.

So, although I was not allowed to be a man of colour in that schooling environment, although I had to perform and act as if I was less than my white counterparts, be they students or teachers, I started to find within myself the spring water of survival which would allow me to stay alive to this day. For me at that point there was no talking about racism within my family and also there was no space anywhere else to explore what it was like to be a solitary Black child in a majority white school. Teachers did not understand back then in the 1980s, or maybe I should change that to, they did not want to understand, because they themselves held racist views about the positions of Black students. It was no surprise that both students of colour left at 16, myself and the other boy, to find our own ways through life, however we might best do so. And whilst I do not know what happened to that other student, I know that my own route, whilst being far more difficult to get to the place that I am right now, was moulded and formed as much by having to survive the racism of school days as it was to rediscover the parts of myself that had become internalised, repressed, and hidden away.

Summary

This chapter, 'The Trauma of Racism', has built upon the phenomenological construct of racism as presented in Chapters 1 and 2. Because we have seen the many ways in which racism can occur, and because as counsellors and psychotherapists our work is to assist our clients, not so much in getting past and over the experiences of racism, but as in helping them to survive the internalisations of racist incidents, which will act out from within their psyches, having greater bravery in approaching these therefore becomes a core part of our work as counsellors and psychotherapists, as explored in this very chapter.

The next chapter, Chapter 4, 'The Somatising of Racism', takes this to another stage. As already explored in earlier chapters, we have looked at the neurological, psychological, and traumatic impact of racism, but if we are going to look at race, racism, and the body, and the physical parts of ourselves, we also have to look at how we can work with the more embodied experiences as they become internalised.

References

Aboud, F. E. (1988). *Children and prejudice*. Basil Blackwell.

Aboud, F. E. (1993). The developmental psychology of racial prejudice. *Transcultural Psychiatric Research Review, 30*, 229–242. https://doi.org/10.1177/136346159303000303

Akbar, N. (1984). *Breaking the chains of psychological slavery*. New Mind.

Albert, A. (2021). *Racism in nurseries: Black babies hardly picked up and left in dirty nappies for hours*. Daynurseries.co.uk. www.daynurseries.co.uk/news/article.cfm/id/1652649/Black-lives-matter-and-children-suffer-racism

Alford, C. F. (2006). Melanie Klein and the 'Oresteia Complex': Love, hate, and the tragic worldview. *Cultural Critique, 15*(15), 167. https://doi.org/10.2307/1354184

Aristotle (2008). *Physics*. Oxford University Press.

Angelou, M. (1984). *I know why the caged bird sings*. Virago.

Bailey, M., & Trudy. (2018). On misogynoir: Citation, erasure, and plagiarism. *Feminist Media Studies, 18*(4), 762–768. https://doi.org/10.1080/14680777.2018.1447395

Bell, V. (1999). Mimesis as cultural survival: Judith Butler and anti-semitism. *Theory, Culture and Society, 16*(2), 133–161.

Beresford, B., Carter, T., Noyce, P., & Van Peebles, M. (2016). *Roots*. History Channel. www.imdb.com/title/tt3315386/?ref_=ttco_ql

Burns, J. P. (2023). The great replacement. In *Curriculum and the Problem of Violence*. https://doi.org/10.4324/9781003304722-6

Butler, C., Tull, E. S., Chambers, E. C., Taylor, J., & Ph, D. (2002). Internalised racism, body fat distribution, and abnormal fasting glucose among Caribbean women in Dominica, West Indies. *Journal of the National Medical Association, 94*(3), 143–148.

Ciaian, P., & Kancs, D. (2019). Marginalisation of Roma: Root causes and possible policy actions. *European Review, 27*(1), 115–130. https://doi.org/10.1017/S106279871800056X

Cooke, A. N., & Halberstadt, A. G. (2021). Adultification, anger bias, and adults' different perceptions of Black and White children. *Cognition and Emotion, 35*(7), 1416–1422. https://doi.org/10.1080/02699931.2021.1950127

Cullen Rath, R. (1997). Echo and Narcissus: The afrocentric pragmatism of W. E. Du Bois. *The Journal of American History, 84*(2), 461–495.

Davis, D. (2005). Echo in the darkness. *Psychoanalytic Review, 92*(1), 137–151. https://doi.org/10.1521/prev.92.1.137.58711

Devilly, G. J., Wright, R., & Varker, T. (2009). Vicarious trauma, secondary traumatic stress or simply burnout? Effect of trauma therapy on mental health professionals. *Australian and New Zealand Journal of Psychiatry, 43*(4), 373–385. https://doi.org/10.1080/00048670902721079

Diangelo, R. (2018). *White fragility: Why it's so hard for white people to talk about racism*. Beacon Press.

Drazdowski, T.K., et al., Structural equation modeling of the effects of racism, LGBTQ discrimination, and internalized oppression on illicit drug use in LGBTQ people of color. *Drug Alcohol Depend*. (2015), http://dx.doi.org/10.1016/j.drugalcdep.2015.12.029

Du Bois, W. E. (1903). *The souls of black folk*. Amazon Classics.

Fanon, F. (2005). *Black skin, white mask* (M. Silverman (Ed.)). Manchester University Press.

Frosh, S. (2005). *Hate and the 'Jewish Science': Anti-semitism, Nazism and psychoanalysis*. Palgrave Macmillan.

Garcia-Navaro, L. (2023). *A surge in antisemitism in Europe – and what's behind it. New York Times*. www.nytimes.com/2023/11/02/podcasts/headlines-europe-antisemitism-israel-hamas.html

Goetz, J. (2021). 'The Great Replacement' – Reproduction and population policies of the far right, taking the Identitarians as an example. *DiGeSt – Journal of Diversity and Gender Studies, 8*(1), 60–74. https://doi.org/10.21825/digest.v8i1.16944

Hall, N., Abbee, C., Giannasi, P., & Grieve, J. G. D. (Eds.). (2014). *The Routledge international handbook on hate crime*. Routledge.

Hall, S. (1996). *Critical dialogues in cultural studies*. Routledge.

Harriot, M. (2022). War on wokeness: The year the right rallied around a made-up menace. *Guardian Online*. www.theguardian.com/us-news/2022/dec/20/anti-woke-race-america-history

Harrison, A. (2017). *A brief history of Britain's racist sitcoms*. Vice.Com. www.vice.com/en/article/mba49a/all-your-favourite-old-british-sitcoms-are-racist-as-hell

Hegel, G. (1976). *Phenomenology of spirit*. Oxford University Press.

Hirose, A., & Pih, K. K.-H. (2011). 'No Asians working here': Racialized otherness and authenticity in gastronomical orientalism. *Ethnic and Racial Studies, 34*(9), 1482–1501. https://doi.org/10.1080/01419870.2010.550929

Human Rights and Equal Opportunity Commission. (1997). Bringing them home: Report of the national inquiry into the separation of Aboriginal and Torres Strait Islander children from their families. *Human Rights*, 1–23. http://en.scientificcommons.org/58686247

Hunt, I. M., Richards, N., Bhui, K., Ibrahim, S., Turnbull, P., Halvorsrud, K., Saini, P., Kitson, S., Shaw, J., Appleby, L., & Kapur, N. (2021). Suicide rates by ethnic group among patients in contact with mental health services: An observational cohort study in England and Wales. *The Lancet. Psychiatry, 8*(12), 1083–1093. https://doi.org/10.1016/S2215-0366(21)00354-0

Hunt, X., & Swartz, L. (2017). Psychotherapy with a language interpreter: Considerations and cautions for practice. *South African Journal of Psychology, 47*(1), 97–109. https://doi.org/10.1177/0081246316650840

Johnson, V. E., Nadal, K. L., Sissoko, D. R. G., & King, R. (2021). 'It's not in your head': Gaslighting, 'splaining, victim blaming, and other harmful reactions to microaggressions. *Perspectives on Psychological Science, 16*(5), 1024–1036. https://doi.org/10.1177/17456916211011963

Jones, M. E. (1998). An invidious attempt to accelerate the extinction of our language. *Welsh History Review, 19*(1), 226–229.

Joshu, E. (2023). Discrimination messes with an important part of your bodily function, raising risk of health complications, study suggests. *MailOnline2*. www.dailymail.co.uk/health/article-12597755/discrimination-causes-health-complications-study.html?ito=native_share_article-nativemenubutton

Kaltwasser Rovira, C., Taggart, P., Ocho Espejo, P., & Ostiguy, P. (2019). *The Oxford handbook of populism (Illustrated)*. Oxford University Press.

King, M. (2015). The "knockout game": Moral panic and the politics of white victimhood. *Race Relations, 56*(4), 85–94. https://doi.org/10.1177/0306396814567411

Lupita, N. (2021). *Sulwe* (1st ed.). Puffin.

Mastroianni, G. R. (2015). Obedience in perspective: Psychology and the Holocaust. *Theory & Psychology, 25*(5), 657–669. https://doi.org/10.1177/0959354315608963

Mitchell, J. (1986). *The selected Melanie Klein*. Penguin.

Oliver-Dee, S. (2017). Integration, assimilation and fundamental British values. *Cambridge Papers, 26*(3), 1–6.

Ovid. (2015). *The Metamorphoses*. Xist Publishing.

Ram, M. (2014). White but not quite: Normalizing colonial conquests through spatial mimicry. *Antipode, 46*(3), 736–753. https://doi.org/10.1111/anti.12071

RMCH, R. M. children's hospital. (2022). *Adverse Childhood Experiences (ACEs) and attachment. What is attachment ? What are adverse childhood experiences ? Examples of ACEs : How common are ACEs ?* www.mft.nhs.uk/rmch

Rockett, I. R. H., Samora, J. B., & Coben, J. H. (2006). The black–white suicide paradox: Possible effects of misclassification. *Social Science and Medicine, 63*(8), 2165–2175. https://doi.org/10.1016/j.socscimed.2006.05.017

Rovine, V. L., & Rovine, V. L. (2018). Colonialism's clothing: Africa, France, and the deployment of fashion. *Design Issues, 25*(3), 44–61.

Sabin-Farrell, R., & Turpin, G. (2003). Vicarious traumatization: Implications for the mental health of health workers? *Clinical Psychology Review, 23*(3), 449–480. https://doi.org/10.1016/S0272-7358(03)00030-8

Samaritans (2014). Suicides in England, 2013. https://media.samaritans.org/documents/Suicide_Stats_England_2020_FINAL_eONhYYF.pdf

Samaritans. (2021). *Ethnicity and suicide*. www.samaritans.org/about-samaritans/research-policy/ethnicity-and-suicide/

Seddon, P., & Crew, J. (2024). Diane Abbott hits out at racism in politics after donor row. BBC News Online. https://www.bbc.co.uk/news/uk-politics-68562408

Shirock, L. (2013). *Echo and Narcissus: The unhappy marriage of sight and sound in contemporary cinematic experience* (Issue June). University of Amsterdam.

Stone, J. (2016). EU Referendum: Baroness Warsi subjected to Islamophobic abuse by Brexit supporters after defecting. *Independent Online*. http://www.independent.co.uk/news/uk/politics/eu-referendum-baroness-warsi-defect-islamophobic-abuse-brexit-supporters-remain-leave-a7091076.html

Tarr, C. (2015). Looking at Muslims: The visibility of Islam in contemporary French cinema. *Patterns of Prejudice, 48*, 516–533. https://doi.org/10.1080/0031322X.2014.967939

Taylor, E. R. (2009). Sandtray and solution-focused therapy. *International Journal of Play Therapy, 18*(1), 56–68. https://doi.org/10.1037/a0014441

Taylor, J., & Welsh Government. (2021). Review of Adverse Childhood Experiences (ACE) policy: report. *The Wiley Blackwell Encyclopedia of Health, Illness, Behavior, and Society, March*, 34. https://doi.org/10.1002/9781118410868.wbehibs236

Tull, S. E., Wickramasuriya, T., Taylor, J., Smith-Burns, V., Brown, M., Champagnie, G., Daye, K., Donaldson, K., Solomon, N., Walker, S., Fraser, H., & Jordan, O. W. (1999). Relationship of internalized racism to abdominal obesity and blood pressure in Afro-Caribbean women. *Journal of the National Medical Association, 91*(8), 447–452. www.pubmedcentral.nih.gov/articlerender.fcgi?artid=2608441&tool=pmcentrez&rendertype=abstract

Various. (2021). Defaced Marcus Rashford mural covered in supportive notes. BBC News. www.bbc.co.uk/news/uk-england-manchester-57806142

Various. (2023). *EMDRWorks*. https://emdrworks.org/costs/

Various. (2024). *Permanent Exclusions*. GOV.UK. www.ethnicity-facts-figures.service.gov.uk/education-skills-and-training/absence-and-exclusions/permanent-exclusions/latest/#:~:text=Main facts and figures 1 Gypsy and Roma%2C,lowest permanent exclusion rates %28both 0.01%25%29 More items

Weil, A. M., & Piaget, J. (1951). The development in children of the idea of the homeland and of relations to other countries. *International Social Sciences Journal, 3*, 561–578.

Zerach, G. (2016). Pathological narcissism, cyberbullying victimization and offending among homosexual and heterosexual participants in online dating websites. *Computers in Human Behavior, 57*, 292–299. https://doi.org/10.1016/j.chb.2015.12.038

Chapter 4

The Somatising of Racism

Introduction

I have written on a few occasions about the impact that George Floyd's murder had upon myself, and I would like to do so at the beginning of this chapter but from a unique perspective this time round.

> As we all know, in May of 2020, as the world was dealing with the Covid-19 pandemic and major populaces were under lockdown, George Floyd, an American citizen, was murdered by several police officers on the streets of Minneapolis. His murder and the subsequent protests around the United States and around the world, in fact, raised to the surface the spectre of institutional and systemic racism towards persons of colour.

> At the same time, when this event occurred, I remember trying very hard not to get too wrapped up in some of the material which had been posted online on social media. The mistake that I made one night in the two days after George Floyd's murder was that I woke up at perhaps 3.00 am or 4.00 am, checked my phone and saw not only some of the film of Floyd's murder, but also some of the protests and riots that were ensuing across the world. Witnessing this, seeing it before my very eyes, woke within myself, nay reawakened within myself, a trauma I have worked hard to suppress in my previous years.

> It was a trauma that meant that I could not sleep for the rest of that night, that I found myself sitting out on the seafront in the south-east of England where I reside, watching the sun come up on my own, thinking obsessively about what it is that I could do or say to affect change, given this incomprehensible and unjust murder.

As discussed in the previous chapter, race and experiences of racism, when we explore them, have deep psychological impacts. These range from the neurological impact, as tracked through a number of more recent studies, to the psychological impact of racism, which also involves forms of splitting from a very early age as

DOI: 10.4324/9781003508854-4

we are formed by the racial construct; then to the trauma of racism, which can often lie within the psychology of a person and within the body.

This chapter takes this final point a stage further and will look at the somatic experiences of racism and how, when we encounter and endure experiences of racism and hatred, what we are left with is a deep wound within the psyche that can often only be explored and understood through using body-work techniques and creative ways of accessing the unconscious. This is especially important for practitioners who have, until now, perhaps gone for a more cognitive exploration of race and racism and eschewed working more creatively with the same experiences, moving beyond logic to the more symbolic and more deeply bodily embedded ways of understanding said experiences.

This chapter will then explore somatic experiences and look at just what I mean by body work, adapting the work of Van de Kolk (2015) and other key theorists who have in their own ways worked incredibly hard to broaden our understanding of how trauma resides within the body. What has more often than not, not happened though, is the link that this book provides in combining the traumatic experiences of racism to body work.

The other part of this chapter will also involve how we might externalise meaning from experiences of body work around racism. One of the ways I am most enthusiastic about is by using creativity. This is less to bring words to our understanding of racism but it is more to bring visual symbolic imagery to said experiences. It was therefore important in this chapter that the words of the participants that I interviewed for this work were presented upon the page. Their understanding of what it is to endure experiences of racism and of hatred is more important than any sort of validation or assessment I might place upon it. This more phenomenological relational exploration around the symbolic internalised experience of racism is a way forward, I will argue, in helping our clients, from whatever racialised background they might be, to explore more safely what they have endured and how they may have endured it.

Working purely cognitively, I have found, whilst helping certain cases, can often also be quite restrictive and re-traumatising for those who have gone through said experiences. Therefore, to acknowledge the presence and the importance of psychological defences around traumatic experiences such as this, whilst also allowing clients the means, should they wish to do so, to explore the deeper, psychological, internalisations of racism, is a major step forward regarding how we might more safely look at and address these experiences.

In addition to this, as I have regularly stated in this book, race is a relational construct. Therefore, to explore it there needs to be a building up of relationship between not just the client and therapist but also between the client and that traumatic space within themselves. Or between the therapist and their own experience of the racialised construct and between the racialised experiences of client and therapist together.

As Figure 4.1, the racial construct, explores, it is important for us to develop ways of working with the somatic experience of racism of our clients; we are also

The Racial
Construct

Subject/
Therapist

Other/Client

Conscious

Unconscious

Subject/T
herapist

Other/Client

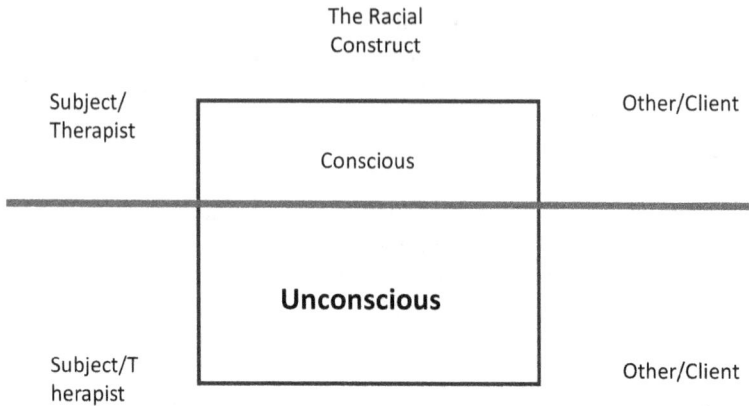

Figure 4.1 Impacts of racism on the psychology of the racialised other

as practitioners beholden to our trainees and to ourselves to do exactly the same thing. The old, perhaps clichéd, adage of *'we can only take our clients as far as we have taken ourselves'* is relevant in this instance. The idea that a person who may be identified with the dominant racialised structures and yet who wants to work with clients of a different racialised categorisation, also means they've had to recognise the power dynamics involved in the between spaces.

To offer an example, in a paper I wrote some years ago exploring Carl Roger's experience of working with a Black client, the issue of where the racial dynamics hindered the relationship between a white therapist and a Black client arose (Turner, 2021b). In the paper, there was a consideration of how, were I to develop that relationship further, it would be as much about assisting Roger in working with his own racialised positionality, as helping to develop ways and means within the person-centred framework that could be utilised within a more cross-cultural and cross-racial framework (Moodley et al., 2004).

This chapter will therefore look at somatic experiences and explore how we might work with them when it comes to issues of racism.

Phenomenology and racism

Stereotypes abound about how we are supposed to look at the racialised other. From the large noses of certain racialised groups to the round hips and large penises. The body of course plays a huge role in how race and racism actually occurs. Stereotypes are placed upon the racialised other, as much about how they look, their physical self, as to their actions, what they might do, what they might eat, and their culture. The body is therefore an important facet in trying to understand racism and in this phenomenological exploration of racism, it is imperative that we actually look at the role that the body plays, and also what it often ends up holding.

Maurice Merleau-Ponty was born in Rochefort in France in 1908 and sadly died in Paris in 1961 at a relatively early age. A man who was very much influenced by the works of Heidegger and Husserl, Merleau-Ponty, however, took a very different perspective in trying to understand philosophy and in particular phenomenology, recognising that the works of his predecessors, and in some ways those that he looked up to, were incomplete (Merleau-Ponty, 1962). The reason for Merleau-Ponty as to why these ideas were not finished was that they failed to include any consideration of the role of the body. Often in his explorations and in his writings, Merleau-Ponty was critical of the idea that perception could only be perceived through the mind. For him, there was an understanding that perception was perceived by the ground of the body, which was then often made sense of through the mind.

This holds echoes in the modern era to the ideas of intuition, whereby an inner knowing is something that we all have the potential to connect with, sits within our physical self, and then is made sense of through a logic, bringing a cognitive understanding to said phenomenon (Romanyshyn, 2010). Merleau-Ponty recognised this and in many of his writings he therefore looked to realign and reconnect this mind/body split which is so prevalent within so many of us.

However, for those of us who were the racialised other, the body holds particular traps and often traumas, many of which we have discussed in the previous chapter. The racialised body is often something that has been misused. This often involved anything from the othering and stereotyping of racialised differences, as already discussed in the early part of this section, to the severing and destruction of aspects of the racialised other which were seen as threatening to the subject. Examples of these include the emasculation of Black slaves during slavery, to the literal destruction of racialised bodies such as the millions of people who were murdered during the holocaust (Akbar, 1984; Cole & Smith, 1995).

The body, therefore, plays a massive role in understanding the internalised experience of racism because it is a core facet of the racialised construct. To develop this idea slightly further, when we talk about race and when we talk about racism, the racialised subject in its definition of what it is, will often project upon the body as well as the cultural framework of the racialised other, that which it deems it is not. In returning to an idea expressed in Chapter 2, around fatphobia, it is therefore the body that is seen as something offensive, as something which should not be seen as the pinnacle of beauty, that therefore leads a whole group to decide what it actually is to be desirable within a white, patriarchal environment – to be slimmer, more svelte, and a size zero (Stoll, 2019; Strings, 2019). The racialised distancing of that more natural, more Rubenesque, more voluptuous, and often darker skinned way of being seen was therefore seen as something which was racially undesirable and the other.

The issue with some of this is that for the racialised other; this can often lead to a form of splitting which, in this case, I will call *racialised splitting*. To fit in with this embodied racialised narrative, using a Merleau-Pontian perspective, there has to be a mind and body split instituted by the racialised other in order to comply with the edicts, be they conscious or unconscious, of the racial subject. As I have previously stated, the messages from the subject, whilst often overt, after a certain age become more covert. These messages which have already been internalised, are whispering their way to the surface time and again from within one's own super-ego. This racialised splitting actually robs the racialised other of their own intuitive sense of being, their own intuitive sense of what is right for them and what is not right, especially for their own body and physical self. This means that any sort of reparation around this racial split, whilst difficult and important to work with, will hopefully therefore realign the racialised other to a sense of who they are in their intuitive inner sense.

Alongside this understanding of who that person may well be, within that sort of racialised construct, there is also a returning of the messages of direction that the racialised other needs to connect with in any sort of given moment. The inner knowing of what it is to be the other, what they can do when they endure other experiences of racism is a core facet, therefore, in this reparation of this internalised split. This is the reason a phenomenological approach, then becomes essential to actually understanding the internalised, metaphorical, symbolic split between mind and body, and also helps us as practitioners to then work with some very interesting and yet difficult aspects of our psychologies that we all have a role to play within.

Somatic bodywork and racism

In his book, *Breaking the Chains of Psychological Slavery*, Dr Na'im Akbar (1984) wrote about the psychological impact of slavery for Black people. His idea being that slavery and the colonisation of the mind involved the changing of how Black enslaved people thought about themselves. This involved the stripping away of their identities, their names, their cultures, their words, their ways of being, their ways of acting, the types of food that they ate, the ways that they dressed. This also involved the passing to them of alternative ways of being, which, although they may have equated to those of their slave owners, were in many ways still seen as less than them.

The racism embedded within the slavery project, by its very nature and definition, involved the dehumanisation and then the subtle colonised rebuilding of an embodied way of being. This is no different to many other experiences of those around the world. In books on his life, Gandhi (2009) wrote about how he was often seen as less than when he wore traditional Indian clothing. For example, when he travelled to the United Kingdom to undertake some of his studies, he was encouraged to dress and be and act in a certain way which would mark him out as being amenable within an English context.

The importance of these sorts of stories is to start to understand our exploration of the embodied experience of racism. Racism by its very nature creates a level of shame about how one is seen, perceived, and experienced on a physical level. The body therefore becomes a part of this structure of race and racism. The fact that so many of these ideas still exist in this modern era often speaks to just how deeply ingrained many of these messages, these millions of ways of being, have endured over the years and also just how difficult it is to see, recognise, and understand systemic racism; but also to start to strip away its tendrils so that it has less of a hold upon the racialised other.

Another layer though, when we factor in the worlds of counselling and psychotherapy and phenomenology is hugely important here. As we understand the body of the racialised other as being seen as something to be offended by, what we also need to recognise from a psychotherapeutic perspective is that the body of the racialised other is something to be projected upon. Building upon earlier statements about the interrelationship between subject and object, when we talk about racism, the idea here is that the body, for example in times of slavery or during the Holocaust, was de-humanised by said oppressors. In that de-humanisation, there were aspects of the oppressors which were then cast out and placed in a yoke upon the shoulders of the racialised other. These aspects were then seen to be unworthy, unnecessary, unwanted, and were then subsequently either denigrated or destroyed, manipulated or put to work in varying means.

Projection, briefly, means that those aspects we do not wish to own of our psychology are cast out from ourselves, and laid on the objectified being of the other, in this case the racialised other (von Franz, 1980). The difficult part of this experience for the racialised other, is that there can be a self-identification with said projection, meaning we become who we are not, or we embellish those aspects the racialised subject wishes to see in us to make them feel safe (Ogden, 1979). This then becomes a form of unconscious racial performance, as we adapt to the perceived safety of said role.

The other part to this is the internalisation of these aspects cast out by the racialised subject. The internalised colourism of persons of colour has a tie to the body because it is not just how one presents on a racialised level, it is also how one looks on an embodied level which is seen as disgusting, disgraceful, and that one needs to change (Veenstra, 2011). The number of persons of colour or, of difference, who crave and ascribe to Westernised ideals of embodied beauty also speaks to just how deeply embedded racist ideas about one's own way of being and appearance may actually appear, as explored in Figure 4.2.

Given that we have already created a link between trauma and racism, one of the most relevant ways of working with these internalised experiences is through somatic work. A concept originally created by Willem Reich in 1933 via a book called *Character Analysis* recognised that there was an embodied response to incidents of trauma (Reich, 1973). Given that these ideas have been built upon ever since then by the likes of Van de Kolk and Gendlin and Levine, it is a growing movement which is busily delving into the diverse ways we might work with trauma in an embodied sense (Gendlin, 1997; Levine, 1997; van der Kolk, 2015).

For Levine, his study involved the exploration of wild animals who had endured repeated attacks by predators and how they managed to alleviate the psychological

The Embodiment of Racism

Stages	The Body	Notes
1	Owned	To be used by the subject. The body is totally given over and subjugated by the subject so that any and all forms of abuse can be enacted upon it.
2	Othered	To be projected upon by the subject. The negative aspects of the subject are cast onto the dehumanised bodiless form of the racialised other, thereby enhancing the subject's self-imposed specialness and superiority.
3	Owned and Othered	To internalise, act into, and to hold the projections of the subject. The dehumanised, disembodied and owned other, enacts the aspects of the subject which it has been told to own, as a means of forming some sort of self-identity (rejecting the aspects of self which have been forced into the unconscious/shadow.

Figure 4.2 Embodied racism

or embodied distress of said attacks and experiences. Somatic therapy which has come a long way since its inception, does a great deal of decent work to therefore explore, understand, and alleviate the embodied experience of traumatic incidents, be they based around childhood, abuse, or sudden instances of attack and threat. Working with the body in this way, though, is not just a Westernised idea. In Eastern philosophies reflexology has, for example, over a good number of centuries provided another route to understanding and healing the internalised embodied experiences that we all have to manage and contain (Baljon et al., 2022; Candy et al., 2020). However, this way of working is something which, although very much embedded within a different culture and with thousands of years of experience behind it, can often be stereotyped as non-scientific and therefore marginalised to a space outside of the Westernised, medicalised mainstream, sadly.

Alongside this, there are numerous Native American practices which work with the emotional, physical, psychological, and spiritual connections that we all have to the body, which involve anything from massage to the use of hot and cold stones on particular aspects or areas of the body (Portman & Garrett, 2006; Struthers et al., 2004). Many of these ancient and simple ways of working work very much along the idea of there being lines of energy that sit within the body and that trauma disturbs these pathways. Therefore, working with the body, understanding the blocks, using techniques which have evolved over time to actually alleviate said blocks, then allows the body to start to heal itself and move beyond the traumatic experiences.

Even within Afrocentric cultures this is prevalent with African bodywork massages, a common factor in the experiences of West and East African cultures (Edwards & Edwards, 2008; Low, 2007). Body work and looking at the somatic experiences and difficulties of trauma is therefore not just a Western experience and is something which has been used for generations to aid in the continued mental health of those who have endured what we now term as trauma. There-fore, when we approach how we might work with the systemic internalisations of racism, and when we consider that racism is a trauma, then working with the body from within these sorts of cross-cultural embodied methodologies makes perfect sense.

At the end of this chapter, therefore, is a structure of how I might approach a simple bodywork session with a client, providing the framework which I will build upon further on in this chapter. The first thing to note is that the therapist should always open the session in a contained way, helping the client to actually ground themselves in the therapeutic space and allowing them to speak about their world as it resides right now. This therefore creates the holding environment necessary for any sort of experiential work.

The importance of allowing the client to guide a therapist in their exploration of the embodied experience of racism is that, because we are seeing racism as a trauma, we are looking very much to avoid re-traumatising our clients accordingly. Explorations of this type should therefore be very gentle, sensitive, and yet hold-ing at the same time. There may be links and ties that we as practitioners wish to make about our client's inner world and their internalisation of racism, which can be explored, if necessary, at the very end of a session such as this. To do so before or during the session, perhaps risks moving the client away from their embodied sense of self into a more cognitive and therefore defended space.

Therefore, to stay with the client at their own path is an essential. With any exercise like the one I have prescribed it is also down to the individual practi-tioner to adapt said exercise for their client. This is not about myself prescribing a singular way of working and therefore rolling it out across the board for everyone to use, this is about myself and my own ways of working, which have worked for myself with my clients, and also that I have experienced myself in my own therapy.

Working with visualisations was therefore an ideal way for myself to work with these somatised experiences of racism. Talking to each of my participants in this part of my research, meant that these memories were often reawakened and brought back to the surface. Asking the participants to then sit with and visualise an image which would represent these somatised experiences meant we could see and explore these experiences of racism together.

The first of the examples is Natasha. For Natasha, her sense of difference arose from the fact her mother was an artist with a Romany background, and her father was from Australia, which left her feeling like she had unusual parents, as everyone else at her school had parents who were several generations English. Her parents' divorce also left her feeling like an outsider, and she hated feeling different to her mother as she spoke no Russian (the main language her mother spoke) and found it difficult to relate to her mother's side of her family. At school she struggled to fit in, where she was bullied regularly for being racially different, and she found no support at home. Natasha developing an eating disorder as part of her struggle to feel accepted by the other girls.

Natasha's story

For the internalised experience of difference, Natasha chose to work with an experience from when she was about 12 when she wanted to fit in with a group of girls but couldn't because her mother was so different to their mothers. The feelings that this generated were as follows:

Natasha: I think I look more exotic. I know I don't look English, so when I meet someone, I'm automatically I look different. I think my name being Natasha that's sort of a foreign name, and all of my girlfriends at school were called Victoria, Charlotte, Poppy, Florence, so you know my first name is difference and my last name is also my mum's last name, because I didn't want to take my dad's name, because of confusing reasons! But that's foreign and having a foreign last name as well you know, which kind of sounds Polish but is Russian, and people would be like where are you from, I'd suddenly be uhm, and when I was younger, I'd dream of marrying someone with the last name of Jones. I wanted to be a bit normal. Now I don't know how much I want that, but when I was younger it was really difficult.

DT: All these things that set you apart, your last name, even down to both names.

Figure 4.3 Racial splitting: Natasha's Image – throwing a javelin over a ravine

Natasha: And yeah, what I look like I think, you know, in terms of looking slightly foreign but then also you know even like I'm quite body conscious, so I went through loads of different eating disorders and stuff and I think my body is naturally quite different to a lot of my girlfriends. I think when I was younger, I think a lot of my English girlfriends, they were quite petite. Kind of like these skinny netball girls, 10 years old, blonde hair and really tiny. When my dad left, I started eating, like compulsive eating and put on weight, and then like not eating for ages and slightly anorexic, and then I went through bulimia. So, my body has kind of on and off changed through the years, and that's made me feel really different. Sometimes now when I go out, my jeans are a size ten which is like a complete normal size for a girl, but when I go out, I will be just standing by my friends thinking I feel so much bigger than them. I don't know if that is a lot of stuff just in my head from so many years of feeling like this and feeling like that, you know, it's just, I don't know.

DT: I see what you are getting at, you're standing next to your friends and they are a size 6 or 8 and you start to compare yourself to them in some way, and that's part of feeling different in some way, part of feeling separate, in the comparison. All right, we'll move on, is that ok?

Natasha: Yeah

DT: Thank you very much. Strangely enough I think I've only asked you one question and you've answered all my other questions already, the positives and negatives etc. Moving onto the next stage, and we're going to do some creative work, we will take one of these examples and work with it in a visualisation like you would a dream, using the waking dream technique. Is there a specific example of feeling different that you'd feel comfortable with working within a visualisation? From whatever age, or time of your life.

Natasha: Yeah. I mean I can just, I can think of maybe just feeling, yeah, I think maybe when I was about 12 when I just felt like I didn't know how to fit into the group of girlfriends that I wanted to be friends with, because I felt maybe a bit like, maybe I'll go with the memory of that, all their mums being the same and my mum being different. Is that a good one?

DT: That's fine, the feeling that comes up with that, and I will ask for an image that comes up with that which I will ask you to draw. Ok. Then are you comfortable to go through that, are you ready to go through that now?

Natasha: Yeah

DT: Then I will invite you to close your eyes and make yourself comfortable.

Natasha: I always cry when I do these things.

DT: Do you need any tissues?

Natasha: They're down there.

DT: Are you sure you're ok?

Natasha: I'm sure I'll be fine.

DT: That's fine. It can be emotional. Then take several deep breaths. And as you breathe just allow yourself to slowly turn inwards. And as you turn inwards just allow yourself to connect with your heartbeat. And when you're ready just nod your head for me. Ok. When you're ready just allow yourself to reconnect with the memory of all the mothers being very different to your own mother. Just notice what feeling comes up for you. Or what do you see? And whatever you experience just tell me what it is.

Natasha: I'm embarrassed and sad.

DT: Breathe down into your body a bit. Can you feel that embarrassment or sadness in your physical self, in your body?

Natasha: I'm embarrassed and sad.

DT: Breathe down into your body a bit. Can you feel that embarrassment or sadness in your physical self, in your body?

Natasha: Like around my heart, I can feel a little bit of pain, I feel tense, and I feel angry and embarrassed.

DT: Around your heart, you feel a bit tense, in your shoulders. Or just in the heart?

Natasha: Yeah, just a bit like I don't feel much below my solar plexus chakra. It's stuck.

DT: Just stay with it, just breath into the area around your solar plexus, and stay with that feeling. And as you stay with the feeling, just allow an image to come up for that part of your body. Tell me what that image is.

Natasha: It's someone throwing a javelin.

DT: Someone throwing a javelin, ok good. Towards you or away from you, to the left or the right?

Natasha: Away from me. Throwing it over some water

DT: Do you recognise the person who is throwing this javelin?

Natasha: No. I don't really recognise them. An Olympic person. Female.

DT: And what qualities do they have, this person?

Natasha: Strength. Courage. I don't think I have that.

DT: So, these are things you think you don't have; strength and courage?

Natasha: Yeah. I didn't think I had them at all when I was younger. As we talk about it my heart just pangs. I feel there must be some real anger towards them. At the very end when you were taking me out of the visualisation, I imagined throwing it at my friends!

The dynamic image of throwing a javelin across water at her friends led her to make the following statement:

Natasha: It's interesting that I had an image, I didn't really think my anger was towards my friends. I thought it was towards my mum. But I think it's a lot also I guess towards my friends for not thinking it's ok that I'm different, you know, like maybe the fact that they haven't been taught to embrace difference makes me angry as I think I have. But I think in that there's difference because I don't think a lot of people are taught to embrace difference, you know. And I think that's why, I mean I do have anger towards my mum but also, I think that she's actually taught me the right way to be as well. But it's the fact that it's so different to a lot of the people when I was younger that's really difficult. But I mean I feel like quite like that's me, and I think probably it is, like quite tribal you know. Whereas they are all in their uniforms looking so kind of, you know, I don't know, it's just like just westernised maybe I feel. Yes, like that.

When we consider the internalised experiences Natasha presented in this scene, it is important to recognise and understand the anger at this other part of herself, this part which she wanted to attack and destroy. When we are racially abused, that part of us which is racially unique becomes a burden. There is a desire to split it off and force it into the unconscious. The internalisation of incidents of racism then leaves a deep painful scar, and we either find ways of suppressing this into the shadow of our being, or we project it outwards onto someone else and scapegoating that other into compliance. There is also so much rage in the image Natasha presented. Rage at herself, aspects of herself, and also, I would surmise some rage at her mother for their difference. Returning to the idea of a double consciousness, as per du Bois, this is obvious in the image drawn by Natasha. The other aspect, the self-hating side to this doubling, is in the ravine split between the two aspects of her being, and the attempts to destroy that which made her self-other.

Nicolas's story

This is slightly different though to the experience of my second participant, Nicolas. For Nicolas's sense of difference goes back several generations. His ancestors were Jewish peasants who were removed from Germany to Hungary during the time of the Austrian/Hungarian empire, but once they had become naturalised Hungarians were sent back to Germany by the Russians after the Second World War. On their return to Germany his family were seen very much as outsiders in the small village they inhabited, and Nicolas didn't even feel he belonged in his own family, siding with his father, another outsider. Nicolas moved to London to be a musician but struggled to 'fit in'. He sees himself as an academic from a working-class background. His differences are therefore cultural, familial, and generational.

The internalised experience for Nicolas involved his being laughed at for not knowing the rules of football as a child. During one game he picked up the ball and ran with it, meaning all the other children laughed at him, shaming him. This experience,

Figure 4.4 Racial conflict: Nicolas's train carriages coming together

in the visualisation, left him with a tightness in his chest and presented him with an image of two train carriages coming together with himself crushed in-between.

Nicolas:	When I stay with the trains, it's very hard and cold and steel and forceful and I'm uncontrollable and unrelenting, unforgiving, inhuman, just no feeling no, unstoppable, breaking, powerful, overpowering, trains it's so heavy, the train it's so heavy, there is a coming together there is nothing to stop that [inaudible]. Much velocity, it's the momentum even at that, it's so grey that they will keep going and squash whatever is in between. Really solid.
DT:	I want to ask you a question, and let's see if there is an answer, if not then that is. What is the purpose of these trains coming together?
Nicolas:	Connecting.
DT:	Connecting.
Nicolas:	They're connecting.
DT:	It makes you smile as you say that.
Nicolas:	I can make an image of the train, the other boys are the wagons connecting and I'd be the wagon, I'd be the connecting bit in the middle, and I'm just completely crumbling and this little whinny kid. I'm the part in the middle that is not connecting and perceives this as being crushed. As not having been given space as having been forced and crushed.
DT:	Alright. Just keep breathing.

Nicolas: It just makes me really sad when I see it. Immediately the image it changes to really Thomas the Tank engine something really quite soft and playful and I can't see it.

DT: Then just see yourself in between the trains, what do you need? The first thing that comes up.

Nicolas: I need somebody to just tell me OK, don't worry you do fit in here. You missed a few sessions and you don't feel like you fit in because you come from a weird family, you're just one of us. Somebody to just kind of pull me up and kind of put my feet on the ground and kind of stretch me out with the, I do have a sense of yes, I belong here, I can do this, I have a right to be here.

DT: Which sounds like that's what you have in the building here, your friends, that sense that you do belong, that it's ok. Like you said the holidays when you are back in this space perhaps, then these sorts of feelings come back in a way.

Nicolas: And those feelings come back at work immediately. I'm not fitting in and they come back. Yeah, they come say here, they come at the row of the houses we live in, really the image comes very quickly that I might as well not be there, not fitting in with this upper middle-class environment. It connects back to the one thing my mum always said was 'don't be in the way, don't stand in the way, don't stick out' which comes back to this family history I suppose.

DT;   You had to hide yourself, yeah, family history, hide yourself a way.

Nicolas: Conform, don't speak out. Also there's, I know it's so frustrating because I didn't go in there thinking that you know I had to, there was a sort of learning for football, I went probably as usual expecting that I had to do that at a grown up level because that was my perception, you had to be able to do things.

DT: Is that work you're talking about?

Nicolas: No, I'm talking about the football. So, so utterly devastating being told off and so diminished.

DT: Then always remember that it wasn't that boy's responsibility to serve, or to show everybody else how it was done, or to do it for everybody else. That wasn't that boy's responsibility at all, that boy was trying to learn something. Like it's not your responsibility to be a certain way at work or even in here to provide certain things for other people, the responsibility is to yourself and to your wife, to those people who are your immediate family. And you know when you, what I hear in this in this whole story is when you've gone back into your own responsibility for yourself you have created a hell of a lot for yourself, and that is ok. There is nothing wrong with the things you've created.

Nicolas: No and doing the weekend group last year, I did learn by the end to be one of those funny Thomas the Tank Engine characters, I did fit in, I played. It wasn't football, which to this day I can't play, I can't even kick a ball.

DT:	Don't worry there are plenty of us who can't kick a football, but to play your way not the way you perceive that other people need us to play. It will be the same as being a therapist, how you choose to be as opposed to being the therapist that you perceive other people need you to be. Understand?
Nicolas:	Where there is an anxiety that comes in from me is that my wife and I are planning to have a child or children. If we have a boy by then yeah it's something about being a father as a role model and kind of maybe helping him to fit in feel better but then I can only do that by being authentically me, but there is something about not having this whole physical experience especially groups of men playing football, there is something in there where you really learn to assert yourself as a man I suppose and bond, and to trust other men and ...

Both examples so far hold interesting facets which relate to the internalisation of racism. Firstly, for Natasha her experiences of marginalisation obviously resulted in a split in her psyche, and an anger at that part of herself which resided on the other side of the gap. This was the same, yet also slightly different for Nicolas. His anger was in the disconnection of the trains, and his labelling of himself as a whiny little kid. The split is still there in the disconnected train carriages though.

The difference with Nicolas though is his doubling here is more conjoined. There is less of the attempt to rid himself of that which has been made the racialised other, and more of a relationship between the two, almost identical aspects of the psyche.

There is therefore the chance of repair when we discuss and work with the embodied experience of racism; that the racialised aspect which has been split off into the unconscious, which has become split away from the whole, as per the examples of Natasha and Nicolas may well return.

Nadine's story

For Nadine this was the beginnings of the case here. Nadine was from a Jewish family living in Wales at a time where there were very few Jewish families, and the only other family in her neighbourhood were markedly more religious than her own. Nadine talked of her family quietly stressing their cultural difference to her from an early age, and of the oppressive nature this created. This led to her feeling like an outsider at school, and to her rejecting her faith during her late teens/early twenties, before returning to her religion later in her life.

The visualisation exercise involved Nadine discussing an experience from a school disco where she felt like an outsider because of comments made by the mother of one of the other children at the party. The visualisation brought up an image for her of a 'pregnancy ball' which was located in her lower stomach. As she said of the ball,

Nadine:	It's almost like pregnancy, and there is a tightness in here, and there's I think this ball, this big ball. It sort of does cover that area too, a big

Figure 4.5 Racial potential: Nadine's pregnancy ball

ball of sadness. The pregnancy ball is like a sort of universe, it's almost like a globe, a soft globe, and It's heavy, its mottled and rich, its soft, it's a sort of potential, I think the fact it is a pregnancy means that it's a potential.

DT: If there was a message that this ball had for you then what would that be?

Nadine: I was here all the time. And that now feels ... I've been here all the time. And that makes me feel very sad. That was it, I'm not sure if anything else came out. It's sort of you know, universal, will probably be darker. [inaudible] full of potential. Lots of good stuff. This feels really good to do. How much time have I got?

DT: You've got plenty of time. You look like you're enjoying yourself there.

Nadine: I am. It's much more beautiful than that, but that's the sort of, the idea.

DT: It's the world, with lots of beauty in there but also lots of dark bits.

Nadine: Yeah, all kind of. There's lots of sea actually. Yeah, that's right.

DT: Ok, is there anything else you'd like to say about it

Nadine: The fact it's a pregnancy, a pregnancy basically, it's a life, it's the life, the potential, and it makes me feel like that life, I think I'm sort of thinking of now, but that life was sort of stunted really, it was made to be pushed into a corner, made to feel wrong, and actually it's so wonderful, the universal wonderfulness of being.

DT: All the potential?

Nadine: The potential. So yeah, I'm sad I'm only now starting to tap into some of this, and that I wasn't recognised, that wasn't recognised, but maybe this bit was, the musical bit, the warm bit but the whole of me wasn't recognised, I wasn't born really, I was still a lump, I was sort of, I was waiting to be born.

For Nadine, the ball's potential, even though it was tinged with sadness, was what she had internalised from the experience of being the outsider in her school peer group. She saw the hope in the ball, the hope to be something more than she was labelled.

The somatic experiences of racism

The images, and the words, and the experiences, of all three participants in this research, each in their individual way, speak of the embodied internalisations with which this chapter is particularly concerned and holds echoes of Merleau-Ponty's ideas around mind and body splitting. We have already looked at how the trauma of racism may well create the split but all three of these examples here highlight just how powerful, painful, and deeply destructive this split actually is. For example, for Natasha this type of split actually has a fairly violent edge to it. The fact that she is a woman who is stood on one side of a divide looking to throw a javelin across said divide to destroy those other parts of herself holds reminders for myself of the death instinct being activated through a process of othering.

For this particular book, othering is actually a process of racialised othering where, in order to adapt to the circumstances and environments which we perceive as being white specific, we split off and destroy that which has been designated as the racialised other. Racial othering therefore is hugely important to understand here because it forms the bedrock for the experiences such as code switching, which was discussed in Chapter 2, the idea that we all end up performing in a way which makes us more amenable and acceptable within certain environments, the messages of which may have been overtly or covertly delivered to us.

Another way that this may occur is in the ideas of racial tokenism. Tokenism is the idea that in order to change a system one has to find a way within said system and then change it from within its environments (Flores Niemann, 1999; Ocloo & Matthews, 2016). In order to do that though, there has to be an allowance from within the system that this is even going to be allowed to happen. The problem with that, though, is that in a process of tokenism, the system doubles down on its oppression of the other and actually silences and reduces the power and potential of the racialised other to create said change. The impact of tokenism on the racialised other, in itself can lead to a form of racialised splitting, whereby the authentic desires and wishes to create change, environmental, racialised, or greater inclusion, then often leads the racialised other to feel the pain of the ineffectualness of their experiences. The number of times I have encountered professionals, students, and others, be they clients or otherwise, who have looked to do exactly this, and have left said organisation feeling demoralised, depressed and saddened, speaks an awful lot to just how deeply within their embodied sense of self the impact of tokenism has taken them.

The next stage to mention though is hugely important. The movement from that quite hateful internalised split within the racialised self-construct, to one where there is a possible union of opposites is what sits behind Nicolas and his experience as a migrant in central Europe. The fact that actually he was able to find a way to start to reconnect the two disparate parts of his racialised character says as much about the work that he has obviously done on himself and his own sense of rootedness within his culture and therefore his race. Whereas it would have been so easy for him to have destroyed, a bit like Natasha, the ruined, self-othered, racialised aspect, what he has attempted to do and was tussling with is marrying these two parts, these parts which in the imagery are quite similar together so that they form a greater whole.

This is the partial power of working with these internalised splits, yet it is not a psychodynamic movement from a paranoid schizoid to a depressive position. It is more of a movement from the depression of the psychological split that goes with racism to a more hopeful union and therefore growth within the psychological underworld.

To emphasise this point, the ideas of Nadine then hold a lot more water. For Nadine, the *'pregnancy ball of potential'* says an awful lot about just what can come to the surface when one works with the body in this respect. It is no coincidence that in this particular image it is a pregnancy ball in the body, in the stomach, that has been produced here. The power of this imagery, the desire to give life back to an aspect of the racialised self, is what has come through incredibly strongly in this final image, and the power and the weight of said image, together with the words of emotion and the hope and desire of that particular participant, is something which, whilst powerful on the page, will on a personal level stay with me for a very long time.

Although these three different examples suggest a road map towards reintegration of the racialised split off aspects of self, this is not to say that this is a straightforward process. Watching and observing all three participants, and even in the words presented in the pages here in this tome, it is obvious that these experiences are hugely emotional ones. So, whilst we are not always aware of what we split and the pain of the splits that we go through in order to perform to a racialised way of being, to reintegrate and reconnect with those inner aspects of racialised self therefore brings with it the need to be forged internally by the tears of the recognition of our supplication. The pain, the relief, the sadness of what we have lost and how long we have lost it are the emotional responses to the reconnection between body and mind that Merleau-Ponty advocates for in his philosophical leanings.

What is also important for me to state is that there is a realignment in these moments of the embodied psychological order. My idea here is that psychologically, when we split, the mind has dominion over the body, and over the spiritual aspects of self. In reconnecting the body to the mind there is a realignment in that split and a change in the power dynamic accordingly. The fact that the intuitive aspects of oneself are then reconstituted and reborn, brings with it a softening, hopefully, in the mind's attempts to hold dominion over its embodied self-other. What I am suggesting here is not a total shift in the opposite direction, rather a movement towards a balancing act between mind and body, whereby the two start to work together psychologically.

Racism, and the internalised splits which we all endure around our racialised identity, leads us to become any or all out of angry, performative, or inauthentic. When we are on our own, separate because of some kind of abuse, these splits are also connected to the psychological and neurological splits that come with racism, as discussed in the previous chapter. They also explain the deeper traumatic sides of racism represented by the need to use drink, drugs, or an inability to sleep, or to lash out.

Where Nadine held something different, was in her archetypal imagery around birth, or rebirth maybe. The fact that her image held within it the potential to be something more, therefore, means that racism, whilst holding aspects of splitting and marginalisation, also holds within it denigration. Denigration here means not only that one is seen as less than by the subject in any incident, but also that this inferiority then becomes installed and activated within. So, returning to our discussion of racial performance anxiety from Chapter 2, the somatised embodied experience of racism creates this.

We create a racialised part of our political unconscious when we are racialised and when we experience racism. We do no less than fight against our shadow, when we racially hate someone else, and we make them take on and own that battle in their own psyche, so that we don't have to. We create projective identifiers of our own racialised splits in identity (von Franz, 1980). In all three examples though, the pain of the experiences resided high.

As practitioners, as psychologists, counsellors, and psychotherapists, we need to do better in recognising that we too have been moulded into racialised identities. We need to do better at recalling and residing with the felt, embodied, experiences of being white, Black, Jewish, Asian, Indian, or First Nation. We need then to recognise that the binary split we project outwards onto the world is representative of our own unconscious internalised split in our psyche. Otherwise, to fail to do so leaves us in a much more combative, much more dangerous space, than Natasha. It leaves us racialised warriors waging war against an enemy which is really us.

Summary

As recognised in all three of these examples, we have to acknowledge that racism splits the psyche in two; the hatred that we endure leads us to kill off something within ourselves, not so much because of the shame of what we have endured, as the hatred that is encouraging us to do so.

To recognise these deeper painful experiences holds echoes of a facet of this work I explored in my earliest book, *Intersections of Privilege and Otherness in Counselling and Psychotherapy*, but this takes it into a different direction (Turner, 2021a). The sharp nature, the relational nature of these experiences in Natasha's example is so much on the page, as well as the almost phallic pinpoint aspect that also sits within the imagery. This, though, changes with Nicolas, which talks of a coming together of two separate parts if one is able to stay with the painful experience. One of the things I recognise when looking back at these images and staying with the words of each one of these participants, is how emotional and how painful all of these re-visits were for them.

The most hopeful part I have found, though, is in the third example. In an unexpected way, Nadine's pregnant potential when we stay with and work with aspects or race and experiences of racism, then brings to the surface something which has the chance of being borne out of said experiences. In a way, this makes some sense metaphorically. Given what I have suggested in Chapter 3, where we looked at the developmental stages of racial splitting, given that there has to be a ridding of oneself of certain characteristics around race in order to fit in with the dominant structures or to endure aspects of racism, then at some point the coming back to and recognising one's own potential becomes a pathway of recovery from the somatic internalisations of racialised hatred.

However, to stay with these experiences and to work through them, I will suggest, is difficult and it requires something of the therapist, or of the practitioner, in order for them to carry said client towards their own particular end game, wherever that might reside.

The next chapter, which will be the final main chapter in this phenomenological exploration of racism, will therefore look to develop in particular this last staging post. It will look to at the potential held within working with the culturally split racialised aspect of the persona, which has become pushed into the unconscious or into the shadow. My favourite way of working with this will be through the realm of creativity and this will be the way forward for this particular chapter.

One thing I should state, though, in this approach, is recognising the difficult experiences of these participants and the painful excavations they went through in bringing this creative material to the surface. It also recognises that to try and put one's racial identity back together again, whilst the possibility is exciting, is also incredibly painful as well. This is another reason, as stated in the introduction to this chapter, why practitioners should themselves be doing some of this work to repair said psyche. Failure to do so, resistance against doing so, therefore leave all of us floundering in a morass of racialised imperfections and in-authenticities. We are taught very much to be performative from a very early age and remain so, inauthentically so, the longer that we fail to look at what it is to be the racialised other.

Table 4.1 Exploring internalised racism

Notes	One of the best ways to explore internalised experiences is through the use of visualisation and metaphor. Selecting an experience of racism, and working creatively, the visualisation presented below is just one means of accessing the internal world. The notes presented here are for guidance and must be used carefully.
Visualisation	• Using this experience, I would like to perform a visualisation that will take you back into this memory, allowing you to reconnect with this memory by using your imagination. I would therefore like you to make yourself comfortable, to close your eyes and connect with your breathing. • As you breath, allow yourself to turn inwards, allowing any thoughts or feelings to emerge before you let them go. • As you breathe allow yourself to connect with your heartbeat. • When you are ready, then nod your head for me and we will begin. • Imagine you are back within that experience. When you are there tell me what you see. What happens to you next? • How do you feel as you look around you? • Can you locate this feeling in the body? • See if you can allow yourself to stay with the feeling and allow yourself to breathe into the area of your body where you experience that feeling. • Now see if you can allow an image to come up for that area of your body. What is this image? • What qualities does this image have? • Does this image have a message for you at all? • Bringing that image back with you, I would like you to reconnect with your breathing and slowly come back into the room. • As you breathe, allow yourself to reconnect with your feet on the ground, your legs, your thighs, your body on the chair/floor, your torso, your chest, your arms, shoulders, and hands, your neck, your head, all the way up to the top of your head. • When you are ready come back into the room and open your eyes
Additional notes	When the exercise is completed, it is sometimes powerful to draw the image. Then asking oneself (or one's clients) a few questions, it can be important to explore the image as well. Questions can include (but are not limited to): • Does this image remind you of anything at all? • Would you like to say anything further about this image? • Is there anything else you would like to add about the exercise at all?

References

Akbar, N. (1984). *Breaking the chains of psychological slavery*. New Mind.

Baljon, K., Romli, M. H., Ismail, A. H., Khuan, L., & Chew, B. H. (2022). Effectiveness of breathing exercises, foot reflexology and massage (BRM) on maternal and newborn outcomes among primigravidae in Saudi Arabia: A randomized controlled trial. *International Journal of Women's Health, 14*(February), 279–295. https://doi.org/10.2147/IJWH. S347971

Candy, B., Armstrong, M., Flemming, K., Kupeli, N., Stone, P., Vickerstaff, V., & Wilkinson, S. (2020). The effectiveness of aromatherapy, massage and reflexology in people with palliative care needs: A systematic review. *Palliative Medicine*, *34*(2), 179–194. https://doi.org/10.1177/0269216319884198

Cole, T., & Smith, G. (1995). Ghettoization and the Holocaust – Budapest 1944. *Journal of Historical Geography*, *22*(1), 300–316. https://doi.org/10.1006/jhge.1995.0021

Edwards, S. D., & Edwards, D. J. (2008). Jung's breath-body and African spiritual healing. *Journal of Psychology in Africa*, *18*(2), 309–315. https://doi.org/10.1080/14330237.2008.10820203

Flores Niemann, Y. (1999). The making of a token: A case study of stereotype threat, stigma, racism, and tokenism in academe. *Frontiers: A Journal of Women Studies*, *20*(1), 111–134.

Gandhi, M. (2009). *The story of my experiments with truth: An autobiography*. Prakash Book Depot.

Gendlin, E. T. (1997). *Focusing* (2nd ed.). Bantam Doubleday Dell Publishing Group.

Levine, P. A. (1997). *Waking the tiger: Healing trauma*. North Atlantic Books.

Low, C. (2007). Finding and foregrounding massage in Khoisan ethnography. *Journal of Southern African Studies*, *33*(4), 783–799. https://doi.org/10.1080/03057070701646902

Merleau-Ponty, M. (1962). *The phenomenology of perception*. Routledge.

Moodley, R., Lago, C., & Talahite, A. (Eds.). (2004). *Carl Rogers counsels a black client: Race and culture in person-centred counselling* (1st ed.). PCCS Books.

Ocloo, J., & Matthews, R. (2016). From tokenism to empowerment: Progressing patient and public involvement in healthcare improvement. *BMJ Quality and Safety*, *25*(8), 626–632. https://doi.org/10.1136/bmjqs-2015-004839

Ogden, T. H. (1979). On projective identification. *International Journal of Psycho-Analysis*, *60*, 357–373.

Portman, T. A. A., & Garrett, M. T. (2006). Native American healing traditions. *International Journal of Disability, Development and Education*, *53*(4), 453–469. https://doi.org/10.1080/10349120601008647

Reich, W. (1973). *Character analysis* (3rd ed,). WRM Press.

Romanyshyn, R. D. (2010). The wounded researcher: Making a place for unconscious dynamics in the research process. *The Humanistic Psychologist*, *38*(4), 275–304. https://doi.org/10.1080/08873267.2010.523282

Stoll, L. C. (2019). Fat is a social justice issue, too. *Humanity & Society*, *43*(4), 421–441. https://doi.org/10.1177/0160597619832051

Strings, S. (2019). *Fearing the Black body: Racial origins of fat phobia*. New York University Press.

Struthers, R., Eschiti, V. S., & Patchell, B. (2004). Traditional indigenous healing: Part I. *Complementary Therapies in Nursing and Midwifery*, *10*(3), 141–149. https://doi.org/10.1016/j.ctnm.2004.05.001

Turner, D. D. L. (2021a). *Intersections of privilege and otherness in counselling and psychotherapy* (1st ed.). Routledge.

Turner, D. D. L. (2021b). Race and the core conditions. *Therapy Today*, *31*(8), 34–37.

van der Kolk, B. (2015). *The body keeps the score: Mind, brain and body in the transformation of trauma* (1st ed.). Penguin Books.

Veenstra, G. (2011). Mismatched racial identities, colourism, and health in Toronto and Vancouver. *Social Science and Medicine*, *73*(8), 1152–1162. https://doi.org/10.1016/j.socscimed.2011.07.030

von Franz, M.-L. (1980). *Projection and re-collection in Jungian psychology*. Open Court Publications.

Chapter 5

The Privilege of Vulnerability versus the Invincibility of Suffering

Introduction

> Diary entry 5 March 2024: As I sit down and look back on my experiences over the last four years, I ponder the changes that I have gone through regarding my racial identity. In 2020, when the pandemic hit, there was so much in the press about us needing to stay at home, to sit and watch television, to surf social media, to 'Keep Britain Safe'.

Not long after lockdown started, George Floyd was murdered and during that period it became apparent for myself that my own racialised identity had come to the fore in a way that I had not experienced for quite a number of years (Various, 2020). I cannot say that George Floyd's murder was the start point for this kind of racial renaissance around my identity, because I think that re-inception of who I am as a man of colour actually began beforehand, with subtle incidents at work which left me questioning how safe I felt in certain environments; witnessing the horrific response to complaints about racist graffiti, watching supervisees of colour who found themselves leaving workplaces because they no longer felt safe within their racialised identity, and watching as former colleagues suddenly revealed the levels of ignorance and racism that they had towards the racialised other. These all helped me to recognise just how unconscious, nay, racially unconscious about this other identity I had allowed myself to become in order to feel safe.

I was recently reading a book by an Aboriginal philosopher, Tyson Yunkaporta (2024). His work intrigued me to the extent that I then found myself listening to podcasts about his ideas and doing a bit more research into the importance of an Indigenous perspective on the existential world that we live within. One of the things that stood out most of all, and how it related to my racial identity, was the idea that in Aboriginal language there is no such word as 'safety'. Safety, as Yunkaporta explains it, does not actually exist. The idea being that actually, when we live in and amongst a community that is itself embedded within the wider environment, not only does safety not exist but we have to constantly live with a layer of anxiety. At any point one's life might end. At any point we might encounter challenges or trials and tribulations which we had never foreseen beforehand.

DOI: 10.4324/9781003508854-5

The idea of safety though, within the Global North is something that is pitched at us almost constantly. The *'politics of safety'*, as I will call it, is something which political parties have utilised in their attempts to actually obtain votes and to create a belief that only they can make their citizens feel safe from the ravages of migrants, minorities, the trans community, in schools, and any other grouping they have chosen to pick upon during this period (Boffey, 2018).

The other thing that I realised, whilst writing this particular diary entry, on this particular day, was that at times in my past I had self-created a level of safety. A belief that I, as a man of colour, was safe in the workplace, was safe in relationships, was safe with peers and colleagues, was safe as a lecturer teaching majority white students. These were all falsehoods and the thing that changed them all, that made me awaken to these falsehoods, was the death of George Floyd.

The pain of realising this separation from an authentic part of myself was the second factor in this self-realisation. The level of safety, of self-created safety, also involved self-othering; the placing to one side of my racialised identity in order to be seen as safe, to provide the subject with an element of safety, a belief that I am not a threat, that I should be easy and able to relate to. And yet the pain of that constriction, the pain, the constriction, and the distancing, of myself from myself then raced back to the surface in a way that I could not have expected or foreseen.

This would not have been the first time I would have done this. This would not have been the first time that I had put my racialised self to one side in order to fit in, to be seen as safe and to find safety. I was taught to do so from my earliest days pre-school. I was made to do so during my secondary schooling. I would have had to do so in my time in the Royal Air Force and there was no space for my racialised identity in my years of training to become a psychotherapist. The path to racialised wholeness, though, actually involves recognising that I am not safe and that, in order for me to become whole, in order for any of us to become racially whole, be they Black or white, South Asian, or from the Romany communities, that engagement with what makes us unsafe for the subject, but special to ourselves, needs commitment and reintegration.

This chapter, that I have written this diary entry specifically for, will therefore look at just how we can use the techniques of counselling and psychotherapy to move beyond the racialised splitting and the pain that one endures as explored in Chapter 4, to a space where that pregnant potential that Nadine expressed in her story is realised. There is potential in recognising our racial identity, nay in re-owning it, and only by recognising that potential do we have any chance of becoming that which we are meant to be.

Beyond the binary

The one aspect, when working with the racial construct, which holds all discussion back and hinders progress in working through this social and cultural adaptation, is the binary notion of race. Making race and racism about the other, about the binary, therefore, will always make it about us and the other. From the politics of the other, as previously mentioned, where the fear of the other is projected onto whole groups, and where safety is then coopted by the political elite in order to maintain control, seeing the racialised other as a threat to ourselves fails to recognise the projective nature of this interaction. What I mean here is that in building on themes raised in Chapter 3 of this book, the developmental stages of racial identity, the fact that we have a double consciousness, that we hold an internalised racial adaptation, means one way we have survived with this adaptation is by projecting this onto the other. Our creation through systemic whiteness makes us who we are, so seeing the majority answer on the pathway towards change in the external white other neglects the internalisations that are far more powerful.

Moving beyond the binary also involves something more than just acknowledging our projections onto the other. For us to work with these internalisations, we also have to recognise that, in projecting onto the other, we have simultaneously othered the other person accordingly. Any projection is proceeded by the dehumanising othering of the other – the rejecting of their complex intersectional identities, and the reduction of the other down to a core part, a simple aspect, upon which we can hang that which we do not want to own of ourselves. This *racial othering* is important to recognise, as any group can do this to any other group; it does not just happen in one main direction.

To say a bit more about racial othering, the first thing it does is it silences. It denies the human voices of the intersectional other, the subject choosing instead to take up a superior role in the need to dominate those they are afraid of being, or even feel they have been, dominated by. Racial othering simplifies the other, reducing them downwards into just their most simplistic part(s); their colour or some other observable characteristic, for example. Racial othering dehumanises the other so we can take out our own denied anger and resentment upon the other out of some kind of narcissistic sense of victim superiority; that because we have been hurt by said other group, that this other group, all and anyone who looks like this other group, are all 'bad'.

One of the most important facets of a book such as this one is that it centres systemic whiteness as the dominant factor in the formation of racial difference, together with recognising that this human construct called race has many forms and faces, many shades of white of brown of black; with its tendrils reaching into many cultures, be they Indigenous, African, Celtic, or First Nation. So, when we see race as a purely Black and white binary, we remain ignorant to the intersectional phenomenological reality that race is incredibly complex. This means when we attempt to explore race and it disrupt its influences upon us all, all we are doing is pushing our own piece of racialised water off the beach, ignoring the floods flowing up the same said beach on either side of us. Therefore, any exploration and disruption of the racial construct has to begin to recognise the collective experience of race, the said construct within each of our cultures in turn, and therefore how our own unique or collective, our external and internal, experiences of racism are either similar or different. This is moving beyond the binary notions of race.

The intersections of guilt and racism

W. E. B Dubois in one of his seminal papers wrote about the 'Talented 10th' (Dubois, 2023). His idea was that for persons of colour in America (although I am going to assume this would also apply to those who had been colonised), for them to move forward in subjective spaces there needs to be 10% who would take it upon themselves to strive forward, to be better, more than and greater than the other 90% of said community. This would involve the whole community coming together in a way to promote and distinguish a certain number of persons of colour through their art, their professionalism, their business acumen and so on, making them into leading lights for said community.

The danger with this is that this drive to be in the top 10% may be personally driven by a propensity to be racially acceptable to those in the white centre. So, what one also starts to recognise is that, not just within issues around racism and race, but also in other structures where there are inequalities, one of the first things that a certain group strives to do is attempt to be seen as acceptable within the subject culture; be it within a patriarchal environment, white supremacist environment, or capitalist structure, this driver, this force is provoked by their own guilt at not fitting in. It is not so much as if they are pulling away and providing a route forward for a culture, but more often than not what happens is that the guilt of not being accepted within said systemic structure actually pulls them away from their own cultural framework and background.

The reason I talk about guilt here is that we often do not look at what it is about racism that actually has within itself aspects of guilt; that racism is as much driven by a sense of guilt about one's own instinctual intersectional identity, one's own colour, one's own cultural background. To be made to feel guilty for being different, for being the racialised other, then leads us to either other that part of ourselves or, in order to mitigate for an inability to change one's own racialised structure, to make another feel it – we turn our guilt into our rage against another racialised object.

Any attempt to realign ourselves to our racialised identity also has to involve a reset and a reconnection with the systemically driven guilt that we have all internalised. This is the same whether one is of the subject culture or the other. What I mean by this, and I will explain this even further later in this chapter, is that even for those who say, for example, see themselves as white and British and therefore struggle with ideas about allyship, guilt for them will be twofold. It will not just be the acknowledgement of the pain that has been caused towards the other through systemic means and their playing out, consciously or not, of systemic superiority, it would also be the guilt and shame at the parts of their own intersectional white identities that they have had to put to one side in order to comply with the systemic structure.

This is important. Guilt, which is not so far divorced from its cousin, shame, in many ways is driven by the superego (Alonso & Rutan, 1988). In a psychological context, ideas of guilt abound within psychodynamic literature (Flynn, 2015; Mitchell, 1986; Perera, 1986). If we use the idea, then, what we are actually exploring in a way is the fact that when we recognise the crimes that we have committed in the aim of aligning ourselves with a systemic idea, when we have killed off the othered object, we do so having distanced ourself from any sort of guilt for the pain that we have caused against the other.

In order for guilt to be mitigated, for example, within racialised systemic practices of oppression, there also needs to be an element of othering or in other words dehumanisation, which therefore takes us away from any sense of guilt or shame that we have created and caused the pain of the other. When Pope Nicolas V advocated for, and allowed slavery to exist in order to help the Portuguese in their first attempts to establish slavery as a viable capitalist project, one of the things that the Church advocated was that Black people and people of colour were less than human and therefore viable exponents of slavery. Although this was something which led to the suffering of millions across Africa and across the Americas, north and south, this meant that any guilt or shame at the pain and suffering of the dehumanised other was mitigated by such a religious decision.

Returning to Hannah Arendt's (2022) ideas around the banality of evil, my sense from reading some of her writings is that she recognised that any sense of guilt at the treatment of the Jews by the Nazis, even through the most banal and menial of tasks, would have been put to one side through the indoctrination and therefore the absorption of the dehumanisation of another cultural grouping. Guilt therefore plays an enormous role in racism and realigning ourselves. Correcting our relationship with guilt is an enormous factor in how we individuate from systemic racism and start to reconnect with our cultural selves.

If I go slightly further and use even more psychodynamic ideas in understanding guilt, what happens with the emotion itself is that it is divested or separated from the abuser, the subject, and then placed inside the other through projective identification. To say a little bit about projection and projective identification, this is the process where the other receives that which the subject does not want to own of itself, be it anger, guilt, or shame, and then is forced to act said emotion out (Ogden, 1979; Turner, 2021). This therefore loads the racialised other up with guilt that is not theirs. I have already stated the ways in which they might manage this guilt, either by becoming more compliant to the subject themselves or by performing some sort of level of self-hatred which is acted out even towards oneself. But one of the things to recognise, though, is that in a process of racial realignment any sense of guilt has to be re-owned and a healthy form of guilt has to be allowed to come to the surface.

In simplistic terms, the number of clients that I have had in the past who have been through difficult, racially abusive experiences, who have then gone away fearing that they will be made to feel guilty in the future, and inadvertently re-enacted the same types of oppression or hatred towards other persons, suggests that that piece of work from a cultural perspective has not been completed. The guilt has not been re-owned. The importance of this is that guilt as an emotion phenomenologically is not a bad emotion to have. In a way, it mitigates and challenges us to do the best for ourselves, for our cultures, for our peers. Yet, when it is co-opted and corrupted by systemic forces, which act themselves out through the racialised element of the superego, then what can often happen as we try to rediscover ourselves, is that we choose and fight to distance ourselves from ever feeling guilty again.

This is the ultimate flaw in any sort of process of individuation from the systemic madness that we have internalised, and in many ways it is the most painful part of coming back to our own humanity because this form of guilt reminds us of our relationships not just to ourselves, but to others about us who may or may not have suffered accordingly. It means that we choose not to see external others as one huge amorphous mass. We look and try to understand them as intersectional others who have their own stories, their own experiences, and their own relationships with guilt and many other racialised emotions, thereby removing us from these binary notions of race.

The emotional landscape of racism

Figure 5.1 actually holds echoes of Figure 2.1, 'A phenomenology of racism' from Chapter 2. The idea here is to look at how race as a construct filters out through different areas of our psychological lives. The reason I have presented it this way around in this instance is that if we can look at how race has formed our identity, then we can also start the process of decolonising or stripping back the racialised co-option to a more authentic sense of racialised self.

On the very outskirts of this diagram, we have the triumvirate that bell hooks (2016) talks about, of whiteness, capitalism, and patriarchy, which, all in their own individual and collective ways, mould the racialised object. How this happens

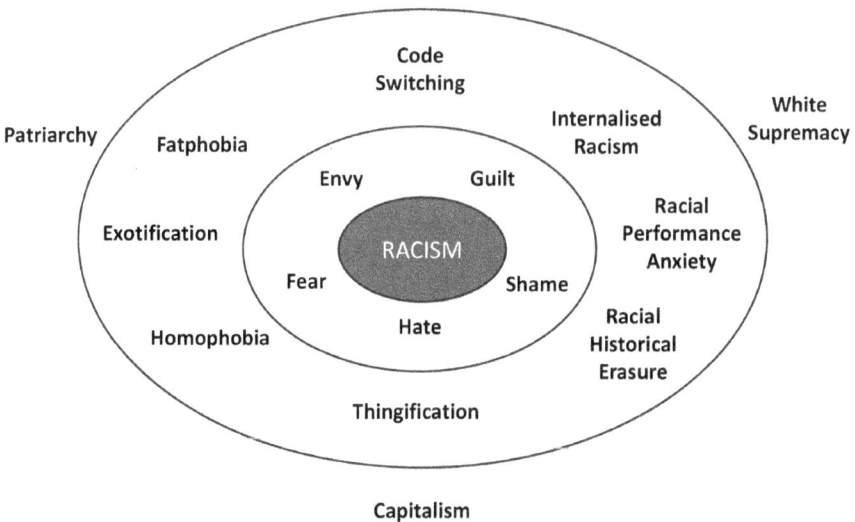

Figure 5.1 Racial realignment

though, is where the middle circle then starts to come into play. Race through white supremacy, patriarchy, and capitalism has also moulded who we are culturally as the racialised other. What this for example means is that many of the ideals that we may have held, were we from South Asia, or from the Caribbean or Africa, are often put to one side or denigrated when we actually compare them against a white, Westernised alternative (thereby bringing with it the binary previously mentioned).

This happens not just on an individual basis but also on a collective basis, where we actually start to marginalise those parts which mark ourselves out as racially specific, putting them down, or adapting them, to fit into a white idea of what our world should be like. This may involve the foods that we eat, the music that we listen to, our tastes in clothes and so on. It may involve types of places that we go to and people that we spend time with. This is not so much about not having a choice, because we all have that choice, it is about starting to recognise that some of those choices, not all, will have been built out of the need to fit in to a racialised ideal.

In Figure 5.1, we do this by being shamed into hiding who we are. We feel a certain guilt that we don't fit into the racial construct laid out to us, we hate who we are, we fear reprisals if we don't conform, or we feel envy of those who are better able to adhere to and feel accepted within the systemic structures of whiteness, patriarchy, or capitalism.

If we look at, say, envy and shame, the educational system is perhaps one of the most obvious examples of this. I, myself, went to a school which my parents believed would give me the best education; a predominantly white, 400-year-old private school in West London. Now, their idea that they wanted the best for me suggests that the schools in their own environments, back in the Caribbean, would not have sufficed for the education of their son. Their envy of the English, together with their shame at their own upbringings, meant that they wanted more for their children, for myself, forcing us into a schooling system which was not built for us.

Yet, this is in no way unusual. The number of minority children who are sent from the colonies to the Global North to receive what is perceived to be the best education, suggests that what we perceive as 'the best education' is something that has been defined from the centre here and actually marginalises those ways of making knowledge that have sufficed in non-Western cultures for hundreds of years. That there is an internalised aspect of racism also residing at the complex core of so many immigrant parents' desires to send their children to the best European and American boarding schools, for example, should not be underestimated.

Racism also has its ties with religion; another perhaps obvious example, whereby often the religions of Indigenous nations were put to one side and denigrated by Western religions and their missionaries who moved into the colonised areas. We see this a lot in the over-adherence of racialised minority groups to Western narratives; for example, the Bible and their near rigid, sometimes authoritarian perspective on these ideas is often driven by an internalised way of being seen as upholding the racialised narrative that has been passed on to them. This passing on, this being handed on to, is often done in such a way as to denigrate those minority groups from within. So, when we have non-white pastors of churches upholding ideals and rules in a way in which their white counterparts may not do, what we will often find is that they will do so to the nth degree and to a much larger detriment to those who are in their parishes.

The racialised aspect of this, of these three so far, also filters into just how far the racialised other goes to achieve said goals within a white environment. As discussed earlier in this book, the idea that when one is marked out as a racialised other, one is then less than, that internalisation in turn drives one on to be seen as equal to, if not more than. The problem with this is that there is always a conflict and there is a sense of a racialised minotaur wandering through the eternal maze of the underworld, never realising that they can never get to the centre because the walls of said maze are constantly moving. For those who perhaps get to step outside of the maze's confines, they are often left to find their own way, perhaps back to their own culture and so on, their journey often being one of loneliness.

To return to Figure 5.1, when we look at the socio-economic status that comes with the triumvirate of white supremacy, patriarchy, and capitalism and how these filter into race, again the idea that to be seen as acceptable, to be seen as successful, as a near equal, one has to climb up the socio-economic ladder. Within all of these there is a sense as well of punching down, a term that I have used in this book and in others, a term that actually denotes the not so subtle racialised co-option of said acolytes to their subjective superiors. This performance of whiteness, together with the punching down of racialised otherness onto groups, or other minorities, even within said culture, is another factor that plays a prominent role in the maintenance of racial superiority.

The central rings of Figure 5.1 are therefore how the drive towards racial superiority plays itself out through different areas of life and in this example here. This is not inexhaustible, they are just examples that I have come across; relationships, the language that we use, the ways that we dress, professions that we choose, our hobbies, appearance, class, arts and music, and knowledge and wisdom. Given that they are all defined from the central idea of what it is to be racially superior in order for us to consider how we might individuate and access the potential of our racialised otherness, we have to start to question how our identities have become co-opted in all these different ways, and many others, that I have not included in Figure 5.1.

Stuart Hall (1996, 1997; Proctor 2004) recognised that there were a number of influences upon these structures which keep the colonised version of race going and functioning. His most important works centred around the ideas of the media and how in many ways the media has a huge role in defining racial identities, plural. The ideas stemmed from the fact that often, as presented in the media, narratives are built around stereotypes and snapshots of the people about whom we are talking. In our comedy shows the idea of what it is to be Jewish, to be Black, to be South Asian, is often filtered through a very white lens and therefore a lens that is tainted by its own stereotypical visions of superiority.

As somebody as eminent, and also as racist, as Winston Churchill once said, 'History is written by the victors'. When we place the meaning of this sort of statement into the world of the media, then media representation is constructed by those who hold systemic power. Therefore, the idea that what it is to be a person of colour often sits around the ideas that Black men are all muggers, thieves, or addicts, and that Black women are all baby mammas, or working in hair salons; these very narrow ideas of what it is to be a person of difference, when we factor in race, holds huge sway over how the racialised other is actually seen. The numerous costume dramas set in the days of colonialism, which show South Asians as being exotic and desirable, be they male or female (often desirable by their white counterparts, I should add) is another form of stereotyping that holds within it a certain narrative of less than, of being less superior to those who hold aspects of whiteness.

As a recent example, the recent Channel 4 Programme, *Dispatches*, based around the traveller communities and their perceived links to crime, was criticised because it held within it ideas that were stereotypical and designed to make those from the supposed majority culture laugh and feel entertained at their less intellectual and more savage cousins (Andersson, 2020).

For Hall (1996, 1997), the media has a huge role to play in maintaining Empire's ideas of white systemic superiority. So, even though it is a tool that can often be used to greater effect to increase diversity, the fact that it is often used to re-create the divisions that are already there is a huge facet in its modern-day power. Simple ideas such as the idea that *Star Trek*, that 1960s programme about a group of fairly diverse human beings travelling through the cosmos, should have within it its first multiracial kiss, and the furore that this raised, shows just how much race and media are fused together (Various, 2018). The emergence of Channel 4 in 1982 and the inception of a range of programmes such as *No Problem*, *Desmond's*, shows which presented non-stereotypical versions of non-white characters, together with many others, which were very popular programmes, shows how important it was for minority groups to finally see themselves represented on screen.

The brilliant *Goodness, Gracious Me* from the 1990s BBC is another example of a show that actually moved beyond stereotypical ideas of what it was to be South Asian, as presented in programmes such as *Mind Your Language*, and *Til Death Do Us Part*, bringing us something which was a lot more realistic and actually showed the breadth and talent within the South Asian communities (Various, 1965, 1996).

The importance of the media to maintain the systems of oppression and therefore definition of what it is to be the racialised other should not therefore be underestimated. In fact, to reinforce Hall's ideas, it should be reconsidered, reconstituted, and reinforced. Race in the world that we live within is something that has been constructed from outside of ourselves. Even ideas of what it is to be white, and therefore superior, fall within this sort of media-driven, cultural, racialised framework. So, although I am talking a lot about what it is to be the racialised other, there is also a facet of this which reinforces the superiority of those who identify as white.

The words of the actor John Wayne and his regular quotes denoting belief in racialised, white superiority, plays into this sort of narrative, as do the numerous roles that he took on, whereby he was not only just the hero, but the white hero rescuing the white female from those who were seen as the other, in this case the Native

Americans (Michallon, 2019). Numerous films have reinforced ideas that persons of colour would only survive for the first 20 minutes before being killed off, such as *Capricorn One* (Hyams, 1978) and many others; whilst the likes of the Charlton Hestons, the Clint Eastwoods, and so on lived on way beyond their demise, also reinforcing the idea of weakness within racialised cultures. It is very difficult, Hall (1996, 1997) also argued, for those who are seen as the racialised other, when witnessing this sort of material on screen, to not internalise these messages.

To build on the ideas of Fanon (2005), racism, as presented in Figure 5.1 is filtered through these many adapted means, and through the manipulations manifest within these five emotions – fear, shame, guilt, hate, and envy. We take on the hate of the subject, and turn it inwards, making us hate ourselves; and we take on the guilt of being the racialised other, making us compliant and supplicant to the anger and need for control of the other.

Shame sits behind the internalised belief that even for myself, the best I could ever have hoped for was to be a mugger, a thief, or something else, of course played a role in the fact that I left school at 16 with no more than three 'O' Levels. In the same fashion, I would be incredibly surprised if there were not a majority of those who have endured witnessing the racialised stereotypical and othering images that they are presented on a daily basis and how it has impacted upon their ability to move forward in their lives; that the readers of this book who recognise their racial identities may not have at some point code switched out of a sense of shame or fear about their accent or may not have dared to read up on their history out of a sense of shame and self-hatred of their own culture.

Within a systemic structure, these feelings are normal, and often we fail to recognise they are present, because we are so used to living with such deep-seated emotions against the self. Yet, conversely, if we want to explore the depth of pain we hide away from, then we only have to turn this around to look at the numerous times and occasions where people have felt incredibly relieved to have seen somebody of racial similarity to them in the media, and how much it has meant to them to recognise that this shift in positioning is incredibly important for those who are the racialised other.

But there is a route forward here, because although these sorts of scripts and this regular media reinforcement take a huge toll on those on either side of the racialised binary, in order for us to move away from said binary, we also need to understand that there is a way to move beyond it to a more intersectional experience of what race, this social construct, actually means for ourselves. This is through the pathway of individuation.

Individuation and race

Individuation through the words of Carl Jung becomes a problematic term if primarily because of Jung's own racism and antisemitism (Samuels, 1994). This is not to say that we should dismiss the idea of individuation as a concept, as a way forward, but rather that, in order for us to understand it, we need to see it as something separate but also connected to the person who created it and who came across it. This is whilst also recognising that, for many of us who live a life of psychological growth, the drive to actually become more than we were actually designed to be, or taught to be, or told to me, by our racial superiors, is one which is inherent to that movement towards psychological growth.

Individuation in this process here becomes a movement away from the binary notion of white versus Black, whereby all who are white are seen as bad and all who are Black are seen as good (or vice versa), to one whereby race, that social construction designed for oneself, becomes something that is self-designed and experienced from within (Stein, 2005; Tyagi, 2008). This is not to say that this process of individuation, and therefore racialised individuation, is an easy one.

In the works of Dr Brewster (2020, 2023) and her exploration of the dreams of the racialised other, among the things that she recognised was the difficulty in actually exploring this sort of racialised material. However, her work does also recognise the depth and connection to source and therefore to the ancestral that goes with said exploration, were it to happen appropriately. Therefore, as counsellors and psychotherapists, to start to look at individuation as a way of working with the pregnant potential placed within us through that predefined racialised splitting, as it is called in Chapter 4, then becomes a way forward in actually helping us to re-take control of what it is to be racialised.

Whilst I offer this with a level of hope, this does not mean that it is easy, as my explorations further on will actually dictate. It is also important to recognise that, through this process of individuation, I am not saying that we can actually rid ourselves of the overseer's shackles of racialised constriction, given that the social constructions have endured for an incredibly long time. It is rather that, as we start to recognise the fact that we are constrained by said social constructions around race and in order for us to explore, express, and work through them, there has to be a going inwards and a stripping back of that racialised structure to something that is therefore more honest, more true to oneself, and more individuated from the binary.

Yet, within any sort of exploration like this, within any sort of individuation away from said structure, there will aways be an internalised, sometimes egoic, resistance to going any further. At times it will feel safer or more comfortable to reside within said structure and avoid the changes which may come with a process of individuation. There is, if I turn to the words of Fanon, Memmi, and other theorists who critique not only the colonisers, but also those who have become colonised, a comfort that comes from knowing who one actually is (Fanon, 2005; Memmi, 1974). The problem with this, echoing the ideas of Hegel (1976), is that, although this process is given to us from outside, and there is a comfort in knowing where one is as the master or the racialised slave, to stretch beyond these confines, these constructs, these constrictions then leaves one potentially in a space of existential anxiety.

The comfort of an identity is its trap; and that is no different when we factor in race. The fact that my father knew that he could buy a suit off the rack at Saville Row for evermore and this would make him seem and look like a good, young, Englishman, gave him a level of comfort, at least temporarily. It formed his identity, an identity that he was loathe to give up, so much so that my father, who is currently in his nineties, could still fit into said suit some 70 years later. And yet, within this seeming comfort, there will always be aspects, slivers, microaggressions, which will trigger the identity crisis within the racialised other that will hopefully wake them up.

Putting this simplistically, no matter how much one performs or code switches into whiteness and its perceptions, there will always be moments, and one does not know when they will be or how they will occur, where the microaggressions of the subject will strip away and remind the racialised other of its difference and its inferiority. This is the problem, the trap, with believing that one is secure within said identity, because that security, as dictated by Hegel, is given to oneself with a caveat, always with a caveat. So, only when we start to challenge the structure, only when we start to look beyond said caveat, do we then start to recognise that we were always unsafe, that this social construction of identity was always fragile. And only then do we begin to see that, in order for us to find any sense of solidity, it has to come not from without, where the culture, the systemic way of living and being within this patriarchal, white supremacist, capitalist environment, defines who we are.

A mirage of security arises when we are externally validated, versus the greater solidity and comfort with unsafety that comes with sitting with the internalised messaging, nay the internalised racialised messaging of our ancestors, our forebears, mothers and so on. This is the process of individuation and this is the importance of individuation because, through this process we move beyond the performative and psychologically damaging nature of the racialised construct, to a place with, hopefully, a more instinctual and therefore more psychologically inspiring and informative connection with a collective understanding of what it is to be the racialised other. All aspects of who we are, of who we have been, come together, informing and giving us notification of who we could be as the racialised other.

Figure 5.2 brings in the next stage of this process of individuation. Although appearing to show that whiteness and the racialised other are separate entities and

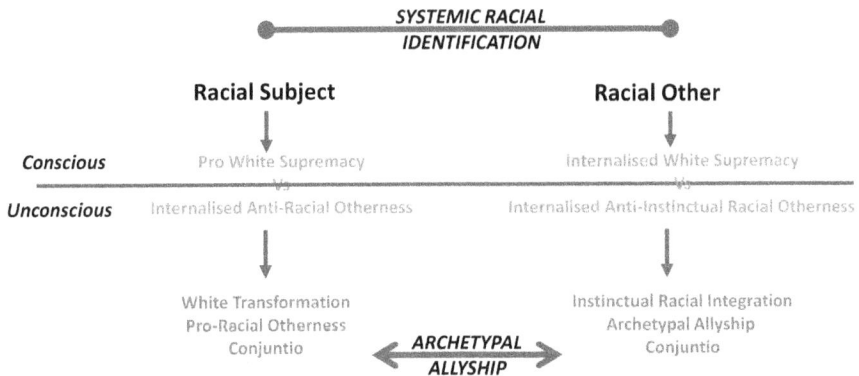

Figure 5.2 Racial individuation

separate pathways, it actually recognises that both pathways need to be transversed by the racialised construct in order for individuation to fully take place. What I mean by this is that often, when we explore issues of race and racism, what we see is a narcissistic attempt to present oneself as either the subject and therefore the other as the object, or oneself as the object and the other as the subject, which needs to give up its power.

I use the phrase narcissism here to echo a point raised by Jessica Benjamin (1998) who recognised that in this binary splitting of race and racism, what we find is that people or groups will adhere to one specific role or position above and beyond any other. This positioning therefore either becomes an expression of one's own powerlessness, hence a type of vulnerable narcissism, or an expression of one's own sense of omnipotence, therefore grandiose narcissism (Besser & Priel, 2010; Krizan & Johar, 2012). To disrupt the projected binary, the recognition, therefore, that we hold both subject and object within ourselves, around this racialised construct, is a core facet to any process of individuation.

Alongside this, exploring the idea that what we do in order to over-identify with one position or the other, with subject or object, we will project outwards the other aspect on to a group or an individual. Given that race, as a social construct, is often seen as binary, this then makes some sense and is part of the reason, when we actually do any sort of work around race and racism, that this proves so incredibly difficult. Ideas of Diangelo on white fragility centre themselves around the idea of a white, racialised construct that when encountered with its own racism feels fragile at the re-awakening of its own projections upon the racialised other (Diangelo, 2018). By the same token, the numerous books and tomes by persons of colour or persons of racialised difference, who see the only route forward as being one whereby those who identify as white need to actually do the work to change the racialised construct, actually neglect the way that they too are built within a system of whiteness (Ellis, 2021; Various, 2023b).

What do I mean by this? Let me offer you a simplistic example. The Windrush generation, those individuals and groups from the Caribbean who were invited to come to the United Kingdom and arrived on boats in the late 1950s, did so not only to find a better life in the UK so they could send money home and raise families and so on, but also because they had been seduced by ideas of whiteness (Williams, 2020). This slightly controversial idea has to recognise that those who came to Europe and the West, not just on the *Windrush*, but from the former colonies, did so because they had been told that, in order to measure up to a racial standard of superiority, they had to be more like the British, the English, the French, the Germans, the Belgians, the Dutch and so on, and they also had to internalise these aspects (Schubert, n.d.; Thomas, 2013). The other part to this transition towards whiteness would have also involved the giving up and the disavowal of their cultural heritage and their racialised otherness. Whiteness therefore became something seductive for so many migrants coming to this country in my parents' generation.

Therefore, to persist in any process of individuation from this racialised construct, we then have to recognise the internalised aspect of whiteness that sits within all of us, whether South Asian, Romany, persons of colour from the Caribbean or from Africa, or even from the Celtic nations, in their ascription and desire to be seen as more acceptable to the white or the European project. Whiteness in its insidiousness is like a tapeworm that eats us up from within. So, unless we are willing to digest and excrete said symbiote, there is little to no chance of us moving beyond this racialised construct, or even, within that, moving back to how we might have been beforehand.

This is the first stage of any racialised individuation. For those who have retained their sense of racialised otherness, if we look down the right side of Figure 5.2, there is an exploration of just what has become internalised within that structure of whiteness. This will often be an idealised version of whiteness, which denigrates and distances oneself from one's own sort of racialised sense of otherness. This conflict of systemically created opposites, in their ongoing merry-go-round of superiority and inferiority, can often leave one to play out some of the scripts that we have already talked about, such as code switching, colourism, and other such things.

Along the left side at this point, for those who identify as white, or see whiteness within themselves, there is the opposite side of the same coin. This over-identification with whiteness becomes something quite nationalistic if I use political parlance. There is an attempt here to idealise whiteness in its more extreme, nay most extreme forms of populism, something we have often seen in the culture and in conflicts around the Western world. Within that, there is a stereotyping of racialised otherness, but on both levels, there is always the distancing from and the undermining of that sense of racialised difference. Recognising how the internalisations of whiteness impact, play out and develop, and change and grow, therefore, becomes the first stage towards any sort of process of individuation.

If I use an alchemical term, this is the Negredo stage of development and of individuation (Marlan, 2005; Schamp, 2016). It is the recognition of the process and therefore the pain that we all went through in being racially egoically constructed, and that we have undergone repeatedly in our attempts to maintain said racialised distancing or forming of our racial shadow.

What it is to be a person of difference, nay a person of racialised difference, involves within it a sense of shame about that racialised aspect, when placed under the gaze of systemic whiteness. Therefore, in a process of Negredo, there also needs to be an understanding and exploration of just how detrimental this super-egoically enforced judgement upon one's own racialised identity has become in order for it to reinforce that distancing. Shame and judgement are actually a part of the racialised subject experience as well. In these instances, though, for the racialised subject, that part of themselves has internalised an idealisation of whiteness, one that they are shamed into, living out to the best of their ability.

Continuing down Figure 5.2, the distancing from that racialised otherness is similar, although I will not say exactly the same, in both instances. What is different is that the externalised systemic judgement of whiteness actually brings with it and creates a form of stereotypical whiteness, performative if one might use that phrase. A process of individuation therefore has to recognise the power of the system that has defined this and in stripping that away and moving beyond it, there is then a movement towards a more authentic Indigenous and, I will argue here, culturally located, idea of what it is to be the racialised other and also of whiteness.

Whiteness, when you go through a process of individuation, becomes less performative, less idealised. Because initially the racialised construct has in its co-option by systemic whiteness become distorted and separated out from culture, in order for us to individuate and separate out from the stereotypical self-othering ways of what it is to be seen as white, there is a chance to actually reconnect with one's own cultural background in a way that is more individualistic and intersectional, and more authentic to one's own inner drive towards cultural authenticity.

Similarly, this can be ascribed to the impact of individuation on what it is to be the racialised other. Given that racialised otherness was seen as something other, different, stereotypical, and therefore less than, the recognition of that internalised messaging that goes with these experiences of being the racialised other, and the working through that undermining that has sat within oneself, on an individual and a group level, then brings with it, I will argue here, a chance for connection with an authentic type of racialised otherness, which is located within the cultural construct of the other.

As a side note, part of this process of racialised individuation involves recognising that, in its formation, the racial construct is something which has actually in many ways been pulled separate, free from culture. As we know by now, it is a false construct, it does not have a scientific basis and there have been many attempts, scientific, religious, and otherwise, to define race through said lenses. All of these, in my view, are a nonsense. The reality being that, phenomenologically, race is a face of culture based around some very simplistic ideas of what it is to be the other. Colour, class, language, behaviours, dress, everything that I have mentioned in Figure 5.1, make up the racialised construct, so therefore any sort of process of individuation, as per Figure 5.2, has to involve a reconsideration and a realignment of the areas of concern within Figure 5.1. The two figures tie themselves together through this process of individuation.

One of the beautiful things about a process of racialised individuation, though, is that for whiteness there is a chance to see the racialised other, not as something to be distanced from, projected upon, or as less than, but as something which can be recognised in its humanity and its intersectional racialised diversity, because that is what has been returned to a person in that subject position.

The same will also be argued for the racialised other and their relationship to whiteness. As they themselves work with whatever it is for them to be racially the other, in that reconnection with culture, with who they are, there is also a returning of the power torn from them to self-identify, a power that does not necessarily reside in whiteness. There is a recognition, through their responsibility to see the diverse ranges of white others, that actually there is a chance to reconnect and be with the racialised subject within a relational framework that has not been experienced previously.

Working with the internalisations of whiteness and racial otherness, returning the projections of one or the other from where we have placed them, so that they sit within ourselves where they need to be, and then processing them through an alchemical lens, are the three aspects of this individuative process we need to go through in order to gain a better, deeper, richer, more phenomenological understanding of what it is to be this racial construct. The tearing away, the removal of the power to define what that is, as per systemic whiteness, as I have stated, creates a much richer tapestry of identities that are no longer performative, which have a richness and realness to them that brings with it connection to oneself and to the other accordingly.

The importance, therefore, of the conjunction of Figures 5.1 and 5.2 needs to be recognised. There is a power in the pathways here. So, unless we are willing to go through the pain of recognising, nay of self-recognising, just what this means, then all we are going to do is continually project outwards that part of our racialised construct that we have either been taught not to own or are unwilling to regain and recollect within ourselves.

One of the richest stages, though, for this process, and this is correct for both sides of that racialised construct, is that it reconnects us with our ancestral meaning of what it is to be a human. This is something that Brewster (2023), in her work on the racial complex and also on the dreams of the racialised other, recognised in her work – that working unconsciously with this racial construct, with this racial complex, then becomes a way towards individuation, process, and growth. What my chapter though, has done, as has much of this book, is seen that actually these social constructions of race in their flimsy ability to have so much control over ourselves, although potentially painful to move beyond, have within them flaws in their construct, which means that the challenge, and therefore the removal, are possible. This means that any movement forward for the individual who is pained by such a construct is not impossible and in fact for so many of us, especially in the modern era, this movement forward is actually desirable.

The next part of this process becomes a personalised one, whereby the dreams that I talked about earlier in this chapter will mark out some of the varying stages that recovery from the impact of racism entails. I have titled these 'The invincibility of suffering', and 'The privilege of vulnerability'.

The invincibility of suffering

Racism invokes suffering. Given what we have explored thus far in Chapters 2, 3, and 4, the many phenomenological ways in which racism occurs speaks quite clearly to a level of neurological, interpersonal, psychological, and embodied suffering and yet, for those who have been on the receiving end of racism, another aspect they are often encouraged to embody is that of a type of stoic containment of said experiences. From the most obvious of examples of where we struggle to even understand what racism is, a part of that lack of understanding is emergent from the idea that actually we do not talk about racism. We do not express, discuss, embody, invoke, or even reveal what it is like to be on the receiving end of racist incidents.

At best, what we might end up with is the stories of artists such as Basquiat, or in the lyrics of songs by artists as diverse as Sam Cooke's 'A Change is Gonna Come' to Nina Simone's many songs on the subjects of race and racism (Clement, 2014; Cooke, 2016; Peters, 2018). Or from artists as diverse as Sinead O'Connor, to The Specials and The Selector and other artists who have often over the years written music based around their experiences of being marginalised as persons of colour, as being Irish, or any other form of racism and marginalisation (O'Connor, 2022; Rachel, 2024). The fact that racial stoicism, which in this case is actually a form of oppression, is a part of this invincibility of suffering when combined with the artists' need for expression, then helps us to recognise that these experiences, these very difficult experiences, cannot be fully placed to one side. They have to find their way out, their way through the body, the physical sense of self, the psychological – otherwise the person on the receiving end will psychologically self-destruct, in my opinion.

The other part to it, another side if you will, is that for many the ability to survive and endure the slings and arrows of racism's (mis)fortunes actually becomes a badge of honour and of worth. From the days where slaves in their varying abusive de-humanisations were valued based upon their ability to endure said suffering whilst on the slave block in the marketplace, a racialised person's worth is often attributed to the amount of suffering they can endure. Racial suffering is a part of this, so the more invincible one appears, then the more likely it is that that person, that entity, will find a way of being within the subject environment.

In many ways this invincibility is what sits behind such things as code switching, as colourism, and so many other forms of racial psychological adaptation. For example, with colourism the painful physical experiences that persons of colour often go through in the bleaching and whitening of their skin, an endurance that often goes unrecognised and not seen, speaks to some of this ability to force through, to push through, to endure the pain of the internalised racist that wanted to be more like the subject racialised characteristics. Racism is suffering and racism is endurance of said suffering. The importance, as discussed in Chapters 1 and 2 of this book, and in many others, in their expressions of stories of what it is to be the racialised other, begins to turn the page and reveal the levels of suffering that persons of racialised difference endure.

What it also does, though, is give back a voice that those who are suffering have often had taken away. 'Suffering in silence' is an incredibly pertinent phrase in this instance. A very Eurocentric quote, it speaks an awful lot to the experiences of minorities, be they women in a Western patriarchal society or those who are the racialised other in a capitalist, white supremacist, patriarchal world. 'Suffering in silence' in a way is as oppressive a phrase as any other I could have provided the reader within this text, because it speaks of the awfulness of the internalised oppressor's hold over the racialised object; the failure to recognise that suffering in silence actually takes away from the forelived experience of what it is to be the marginalised other, the working class other, the racialised other, for this book, in a white, patriarchal, capitalist world.

The returning of the voice and the breaking down of that internalised racial stoicism, these two aspects then start to rebuild the humanity of the racialised other and return to it that sense that it has a right to be seen and to be respected. These are, however, nothing less than the ways and means by which we actually then all repress those aspects of ourselves which we struggle with having seen in the wider world. As already discussed, a core theme of this particular chapter is to look at just how deep the repressions go through the lens of dream work.

Dream dated 20 February 2023

A scene where I am in a building with an old, wise man who is in the basement in the kitchen. I go to some other part of the basement and in my parents' room a Black man is being taken away. Two daleks appear, though when I rush to hide behind the door in the kitchen, they come in and then they take the old man away as well. They turn off the lights. I sneak out after they have gone and I go up two flights of stairs until I get to my childhood bedroom before James, from the CCPE arrives. I hide on the balcony as James enters with two other prominent white men. I then come back in and ask for quiet as James speaks to the daleks in the building.

This dream speaks of the internalisations of whiteness that I have already discussed in this chapter. The only other persons of colour in the dream are the person in the bedroom down in the basement and the wise, older man. Every other character in the dream is white. The part though, the destructive, hateful part of my own psyche is held within a character from an old television show I used to love and enjoy when I was a child. The daleks created by Terry Nation back in the early 1960s were a part of a programme called *Doctor Who* (Various, 2023a).

Without going into too much detail around the programme itself, other than saying that this programme is very much built around the idea of white saviourism, one of the core facets about the daleks and in particular how they were created is that they were there to represent something akin to the Nazi ideal. In the show, their creator, named Davros, in genetically modifying his own race, had come up with a perfect organism, full of hate and devoid of emotions, and encased said organism within a metal construct. The organism's eternal pain and hatred were harnessed and then projected outwards on to other races and creatures around the universe which they were then supposed to subjugate, destroy, and conquer. They were the ultimate dominating machine.

The dream therefore speaks to this self-domination, this self-immolation of my own racial identity and it also speaks to the fear that I often used to have about my own racial identity.

Another minor part to this particular dream is the date that I had it. The original ideas for this book were actually birthed in January and February 2023, so therefore to have a dream tracking my own sort of process during this period of time makes a type of cognitive and psychological sense. The fear within my own self to speak about what it is to be the racialised other, the fear that I might speak up and therefore be annihilated from without or even from within, hence the daleks, is there within the dreamscape.

Dream dated 27 February 2023

> This is a scene where I am an escaped slave alongside some other slaves. We are all trying to cross a swamp but being hunted by white and Black men with guns. As some of my friends are caught, I back away again through a layer of netting in the swamp and I hide. However, one of the men sees me hiding in the netting, fires a gun and misses. I escape but not before one of the overseers says something about a slave being raised in Perth Australia. I say, 'I know' and then I decide that I want to fly there, my idea being that I want to be the first Black escaped slave to travel to Australia. I then find myself going down a series of floors as I try and escape.

This dream moves on from the original one. As already expressed, in any sort of movement whereby we decolonise our own psyche from the impact of systemic racism, there has to be a recognition that that which silences us, that which has us code switching, that which has us wanting to change who we are in order to fit in with the systemic, racialised environment that we live within, is not always enforced from outside. Yes, it has been internalised from outside but in our own failure to recognise that not only do we live within racist environments, that we are said environments, that this part sits within us and is active at all times.

There are the pursuers in the dream. They are not just white; they are also Black. The combination of the two therefore speaks to systemic, internalised racism. The pain of watching other slaves being re-captured, taken away in order to endure their captivation back on the plantations of my internalised world is still there, however. But there is also a hint of a way out in this dream. The hearing from one of the overseers that actually there is freedom in Australia, although helpful in this context from my own particular dream, speaks to the journey being southward from wherever I am residing in captivity. There is an immense amount of pain and distress in this dream as well as fear, the fear of having to run and free oneself. In some ways I would say fear is too mild a word, I think there is actually real terror, given the fate of quite a few slaves during this time.

The hatred of the overseers is there, as it is in the previous dream in the hatred of these mechanical beings, the daleks. What there is not is a sense of envy, although I wonder where that might be in some ways and the only people to actually speak up in both these two early dreams are those who are white. In the first dream I do not have a voice, but in this one, I begin to find my voice. Even if this is only in the utterance of two words. There is the beginning of the breaking of this invincibility of silence, about which I have already spoken. In both dreams, though, I endure the suffering, the pain, the rejection, the outsiderness that comes with being the racialised other.

To say a couple of final things about this particular stage of dream work. The invincibility of suffering, although present in both dreams, also speaks of an attempt and a desire for something more, for something different. The old, Black man in the kitchen in the basement speaks of something, I could argue, more intuitive, wiser, more archetypal, or ancestral if I go down the route that Dr Brewster might follow. It is there and it is taken away by the mechanical, internalised sense of whiteness. By the same token, in this particular dream, there is a whispering of a way out towards a culture that has its roots very much situated within ancestral norms and stories. Both of them speak to a way out. Both of them hint at something which, at that particular point of this particular process, the writer, myself was not able to access.

To offer another perspective on the importance of the racialised other challenging their invulnerability, it is probably worth just moving sideways into the world of toxic masculinity. Toxic masculinity (Haider, 2016) is a term used to denote the systemic injunctions placed upon men, regarding their behaviour, actions, and how they are supposed to be in the world. Things such as vulnerability, emotions, tears, sadness, and so on are considered unworthy of a man within such environments. The fact that this system of toxic masculinity has endured for so long talks about how systemically it is held, not just by men, but also by a sizeable number of women as well.

Toxic masculinity though, has a darker, shadowy side. It is something that has led to the deaths through suicide and other means of a considerable number of people across the Global North. Toxic masculinity is also something that has impacted on men and women within the LGBTQ communities, meaning that often, because men are siloed into a certain way of being, anything that sits outside of it is denoted as gay, homosexual, butch, or stereotyped in some way, which is not at all helpful and can be quite detrimental to the mental health of those who genuinely exhibit differing behaviours (Hunt et al., 2021; Lick et al., 2013; Troya et al., 2022).

Toxic masculinity at its core speaks to the invulnerability of men, an invulnerability that dehumanises said men in order that they may perform certain duties, such as anything from working long hours in the workplace to going to the front line in war time. This also suggests something about the nature of being used as a man, the dehumanisation of toxic masculinity, just like the dehumanisation of system internalised racism actually leaves the racialised other, as it does with men, less than human, less complete, and more able to be manipulated by those who purport to be part of the systemic majority.

Returning to the idea of how this fits in with racism, the invincibility of suffering then holds echoes of the same invincibility of masculinity that is projected through male culture. We often see a similar ethos placed within the racialised other on sports fields, for example. The idea that if you are the racialised other, you should be the best at anything from cricket, to football, to rugby, to American football, to some sport somewhere along the way. None of these speaks of the pain of these achievements nor of the systemic racism which I believe at times underpins these drives towards sporting perfection.

Much like the silencing that sits within toxic masculinity, *racial toxicity*, as I am wanting to call it in this book, therefore also has within it a silencing element. The silence enforced from outside of the racialised other means that their experiences are not in fact heard. They are not receiving the racialised other because in order for them to receive it, the subject would have to acknowledge the pain endured by the racialised other as well as feel the guilt and the shame of having caused such pain. Ultimately, any sort of expression of the pain of the racialised other brings with it a re-humanising of that racialised person, collective, or culture and the racialised subject, much like the master in Hegel's dialect, does not wish to see the racialised other as anything more than inhuman.

The privilege of vulnerability

Figure 5.3 changes this narrative hugely. Whereas in certain cultures and in certain environments, systemic oppression also holds within it the right of a certain group to be, to express their pain, their art history, and so on, for the racialised other those expressions of racialised pain, supplication, and otherness often have to be filtered through creative means. *Figure 5.3* speaks to some of the ways in which this pain is expressed. This could be through the arts, music, poetry, and so on – means through which often the racialised other talks about their experiences of being marginalised.

To offer you a couple of simple examples: in 1994 Steven Spielberg won several Oscars for the film *Schindler's List* (Spielberg, 1993). When talking about his

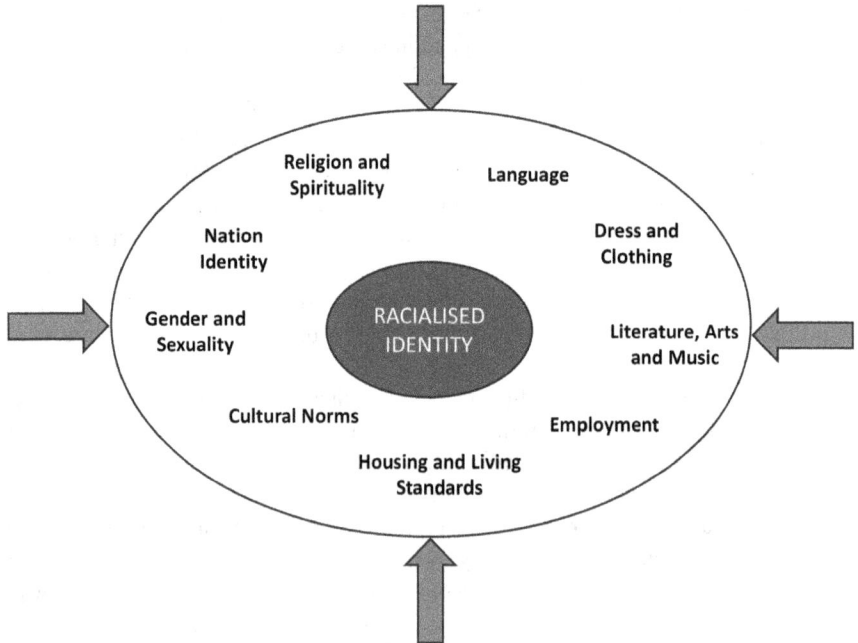

Figure 5.3 Racial authenticity

process of making this film, Spielberg spoke of feeling a draw to actually tell this story, a story of a man who saved thousands of Jewish lives from the concentration camps during the Second World War. This was as much to heal himself as it was to express a much-needed story about the Jewish experience during the Second World War. In particular, he spoke about visiting Auschwitz and how in his visit to Auschwitz he expected to feel a great deal of sadness; but what he was surprised by, moved by, and also motivated by was the fact that he felt incredible anger whilst walking through Auschwitz, anger which he then used to fuel his project and his work.

To offer you another example. In 1963 there was a bombing of a church in Alabama in the United States. Four young women, who were basically just in the church to pray and to commune with their god, were murdered. The murderers, who were white nationalists, were never brought to trial (Kindig, 2015). The artist Nina Simone wrote a wonderful song called 'Four Women' (Simone, 1966). Her drive to write the song was based around the rage that she felt at the deaths of these four innocent women in such horrific circumstances and the continued fight for racial civil rights in the United States.

Jean-Michel Basquiat, the Brazilian artist, would often create images and symbols in his artwork which spoke to the marginalisation that he endured whilst living in America. His work was picked up and understood by other white artists, perhaps one could call them white allies, such as Andy Warhol (Clement, 2014). I could list a respectable number of other more contemporary artists, philosophers, writers, and singers from across the globe who have all in their own way written stories about racism, be it overtly or covertly. Hip Hop music, for example a genre which is very close to my own heart, in its early days spoke hugely to the internalisation and the pain of being the racialised other in America, much like Grime does here in the United Kingdom in the modern era.

The pain of racism and the privilege of being able to express that suffering, is something which, although often denied to the racialised other, has always found its way out through the arts, through song, through imagery, and through stories and storytelling (Bauman, 2023; S. Benjamin & Dillette, 2021). So much so that actually many of these stories have become quite mainstream in our modern world.

So, on the one hand, the silencing of our vulnerability as the racialised other walks hand in hand with the dehumanisation of the racialised other. On the other, the ability to express and feel the pain, the sadness, the rage of being the racialised other, brings with it a re-humanisation of the racialised other, as much for themselves as it might be for our position in the wider racialised subject structure.

This conflict between silencing and dehumanisation and the expression, creative or otherwise, and re-humanisation is not just something that is enforced from the external, it is something that can often be internalised by the racialised other. Performance anxiety, for example, believing that one as the racialised other doesn't have the right and the authority to speak up within systems that oppress us, is just one aspect of this privilege of vulnerability through which I am talking. The internalised struggle based around an external reality is something that so many clients of my own, as well as myself in varying ways, have had to wrestle with over time (Egilmez & Orum, 2018).

The messages on our training courses where I hear a number of students from racialised groups who often fear speaking up about their experience and about their dissatisfaction with their courses, versus being labelled or silenced and having to toe the line, is part of this same strange and yet hugely interesting and important dichotomy and psychological split within the racialised other. Too many of our students who are the racialised other have to go through this process of rediscovering their humanity through their voice and too rarely are our courses equipped and knowledgeable enough to therefore allow a safe enough space where the racialised other can have their story heard and witnessed.

On training courses that I run around intersectional difference, one of the things that I choose to do as part of a day on understanding how to be with difference, is in giving space for all participants to express their experience of being the other. If I was to bring this into a racialised context, then giving a safe space for the racialised other to express their story to people who are not there to '*therapise*', who are not there to judge, and who are just there to sit, receive, hear, and even allow themselves to be at least even partially triggered by the experiences they are hearing, not only returns the humanity of the racialised other back to them and to their soul, but also, in the eyes of the subject, in this case the trainee therapist, gives them the chance to actually hold and feel the pain of another, the humanness of the other.

Dream from Monday 17 February 2024 03:55

> I am on my way to the centre and I get off a bus in the centre of town. I am being followed by a guy who tries to steal my wallet but I notice and as he gropes for my wallet, I take off my jacket, shrugging him and it off and away because I am hot. I turn right into a station on the other side of the road and I try and take a shortcut but a boxer dog is there. The dog speaks to me and says that I cannot come down that way. A burley white man with a shaved head tries to tackle me but I get away from him and I trick him by flying into the air as he falls off the road and into the river. I fly across the river, singing 'If you can't see what I can see' by Heavy D and the Boyz. As I do so, a number of people who are still on the bank of the river give me a thumbs up as I fly towards the centre.

This dream speaks of that internalisation of whiteness which symbolically represents the subject. Whereas in previous dreams in this chapter there is a sense of those symbols then taking up an awful lot more space and dominating the inner psychology of myself. Within this particular dream there is a voice, a song which emerges from my own mouth and rises from my own creativity, which people enjoy and want to hear.

As a brief side note, Heavy D and the Boyz (2002) were an old 1980s and 1990s Hip Hop band. One of my favourites, that is true, yet their music, as represented in this dream, speaks a lot to the movement from internalised oppression and silencing to one whereby I am able to distance myself from that overbearing sense of internalised oppression, shaking it away and actually saying what I want to say.

The second part of this to recognise is that heat and fire and anger are psychological cousins. The symbology of being hot, of having to hold my fire in, is shaken off by the fact I get rid of the coat and yet I retain the wallet. At this point, I no longer have to contain myself and it is the freeing myself of a jacket that actually allows me to fly, to take off, to take to the sky, to feel free. Internalised whiteness goes down into the depths. It is never destroyed, people always reside somewhere within the psyche, but in distancing oneself from its overarching power over oneself, there is a chance to actually rise up, Maya Angelou style, and be that bit more as per this dream.

Dream dated 21 February 2024

A scene where I am in my parents' home in the basement with two other Black people. There is a dalek in there which threatens to come in, so I send my own machine up to defeat it. It fails and the dalek comes down. We hide in the back of the bedroom in the basement, behind some glass. I use my sonic screwdriver to confuse the dalek into a sort of submission. I go up to the front door on the ground floor, where a white man has been secretly staying. I throw him out of the front door and close all the windows before he can come back in. There is a part of me that feels sorry for throwing him outside because I am aware that he is getting married in the morning, but there is also another part which is aware that nobody helped me at all and it was the right thing to do to get rid of this part of myself.

The importance of this dream is that, when we think about vulnerability and the movement from an internalised hatred of one's own racialised identity to a position whereby one feels and is able to be racially more authentic, it speaks of the internalised struggle to inhabit that. As explored earlier in this chapter, internalisations play a huge role in what it is to be the racialised other – the definitions of such being projected into the racialised other, from where they reconstitute themselves and maintain a hold over the egoic sense of self. In this dream though, there is a movement down into the body, into the basement, into the shadow perhaps, of the psyche and through this exploration of the psyche there is a finding of two things.

First, there are the other aspects of the racialised self which one needs to inhabit, and alongside this there is also the weaponry which one might choose to use to defeat that internalisation of the subject supremacist. This subject supremacist in this dream, in the form of a dalek, then finds itself defeated and in the defeat of this sort of mechanicalized super-egoic part of the psyche there is a challenging and a taking back from that part of the power that it has over one's self to define who one is as the racialised other.

The other part of this dream, which is quite interesting, is the removal of that internalised sense of whiteness which sits so close to the front door. Together with this, the sense of guilt, of sadness, and having this part removed, speaks a lot about the co-option of the slave by the master – to use a Hegelian term, it is dialectic. There is imparted within the slave a sort of loyalty, a frailty within themselves that leads them to actually to want to play out that role as the racialised other. That is not necessarily to say that I am trying to victim blame racially, but to suggest that, in a system of racialised abuse, there is part of said abuse which has become so internalised within the psyche of the racialised victim that they cannot see themselves as anything more than subservient to the racialised subject.

If I look at this through an intersectional lens, then we see this most obviously through a class structure, whereby those of a working class or an immigrant class often find themselves beholden and feel a loyalty towards those of a higher-class stratum. This contrasts of course with those who wish to move up the class structures of a community or a culture, but for those who choose not to do so, or who cannot do so, their willingness and their admiration for those who are seen as of a higher-class position to themselves is a form of class sympathy for the subject.

Racial sympathy is a similar form, whereby a certain sympathy is given to the subjective oppressor, be it internal or external, for their machinations. We see it in many other areas. For example, in the days post the 6 January 2021 riots on the Capitol buildings in the United States of America there was a lot of recognition of the sympathy afforded to white nationalists who raided the Capitol buildings, especially when compared to civil rights activists who campaigned across America post the murder of George Floyd (Various, 2021). The fact that so many of those men were at the very top of the class structure in the United States, that so few of them have been convicted of their very prominent roles in enticing and coercing these riots to take place, speaks of an intersectional conjunction between class and whiteness and patriarchal sympathy afforded by the systems that they all reside within. One could imagine, quite understandably, that were these rioters Black immigrants and so on, many of them would either have been shot of have been forcibly removed from the country with haste.

This sympathetic part is what actually keeps the racialised other in a subservient space with the subject. It is important to emphasise the fact that, for all of us, myself included, unless this part is challenged within the psyche, then it is increasingly difficult for us not to then go back and re-enact the internalised racial superiority that we have swallowed whole from the days of our inception onwards. The importance of these four dreams is that they speak of a pathway – a difficult pathway but one that stretches down through the body into the psyche and into the shadow to rescue and recover those parts of the racialised structure which sit near the collective unconscious.

During this whole process, there were other dreams that I could have used for this particular chapter, which also speak of this racialised self-realignment to one's own sort of cultural identity, but it felt important to talk of the struggle, the difficulty, the pain, and also the recognition of the darker elements of this struggle within oneself. This process will always be ongoing and what I often recognise when working with clients around their sort of internalisation of race and racism is that, when we start to explore these symbols, clients start to rediscover their ancestral lineage, and the movement down through the psyche.

For those who identify as white, that shifting of their narrative around what it is to be white is a core facet in rediscovering what it means for them to be persons who identify as white, which therefore sits beyond the cultural construction of this racialised identity. This is very different for those who are seen as the racialised other. In the rediscovery of that racialised identity there is a movement away from the stereotypical, self-objectifying ways in which one might self-identify. There is a stretching beyond the stereotypes of Black masculinity, which will also include forms of machismo and a sort of toxic, Black masculinity which I have written about before (Turner, 2022), whereby what we end up with is a caricature of Black masculinity which actually fits more of the white narrative and the white fears of Black masculinity, than it does of a true sense of what it is to be a Black man. This dream continues the progression away from the binary idea of race as a construct, with its splitting and projection, and takes us in the direction of understanding one's own notions of race, the internal versions.

The other part about this, when we start to stretch downwards and into the collective unconscious and explore what it is to be the racialised other, is that we also move beyond the self-imposed self-othering stereotypes of what it is to be the racialised other and start to work intersectionally, where we start to discover and rediscover aspects of our racialised identity that connect with other aspects of identity, and within this reconnection with aspects of identity we start to redefine what the racialised identity actually is.

To emphasise this point a little bit further, this deep delve into what it is to be the racialised other and this realignment, this change, this shifting of a perspective, this broadening of the framework of what it is to be the racialised other, when we strip away the experiences of internalised racism, then what we start to recognise is that what it is to be the racialised other could incorporate other ideas about what it is to be the racialised other. Identities about disability and how they intersect with racialised identity (Mereish, 2012). We look at different forms of masculinity and femininity so that they are not so predefined and return to, if we are lucky, cultural norms of racialised identity which sit within the cultural framework from which we have become detached in our co-option and adherence to the super-egoic, systemic subject structures.

The final thing I want to say about this shift is that it is incredibly painful. As presented here, there is a movement from outside to in as if this is an uncomplicated process. The reality is that movement from outside to in also involves inside to out and it goes backwards and forwards time and time again. The reasons for this are fairly obvious. We do not live in a space in which we can escape from the media, the world outside of ourselves, and in fact if I return to the work of Stuart Hall (1996) and his explorations around media internalisation, what we have in the years post Hall is the rise of social media. With this shift to social media, and multimedia, and other ways of obtaining information, these internalisations can feel like we are constantly bombarded by messages that tell us who we should and how we should and should not be.

It is incredibly difficult and challenging, and yet psychologically essential, for all of us of the racialised other to be working with those internalisations of identity and exploring how they have become co-opted by the wider, systemic, subjective world.

Summary

As explored in this chapter, there is a wealth of material that clients can access if they are willing to work with the internalisations of race. *A Phenomenology of Racism*, the title of this book, in its exploration of how we all have an experience of race as a construct, therefore allows us the space to actually look at and understand what our relationship might be, or might not be even, to that racialised construct that sits outside of ourselves and also has a great influence on who we are.

Therapists working with this sort of material need to be very aware of some of the ideas raised in previous chapters. If we are going to see racism and the internalisation of racism as something that causes trauma, then hopefully what we will see over the past couple of chapters is that as we start to work with racial trauma, in the most gentle and kind and loving of ways, then, what we start to do is build up a trust and an awareness within the client that their experience of racialised trauma is real – that we not only have the chance to validate it, but that there are ways of moving beyond it so that the pain of this trauma, whilst not totally extracted from the psyche, is something that we can learn to live with.

In the last dream the fact that the dalek has gone and the white man is outside does not speak to the end of a process. What it speaks to is those parts that have been put to one side in order for something more to grow. This is the importance of this sort of stage. Therapists should therefore be working gently with this material. We have looked at working with the body and I have often in my own sort of work used visualisations to explore this sort of material, but in the previous chapter we looked at how we can use creative means to actually explore some of these internalisations and find a gentle way beyond the egoic sense of self and beyond some of the defences that we may all have around exploring this, in order to access, process, and bring awareness up from the unconscious for our clients so that they can actually see the material they are working with.

My final words around this chapter continue my narrative around the use of creativity. Working in a purely cognitive way, whilst possibly helpful for certain clients, may not be as helpful for those clients who have been labelled as the racialised other. When we start to explore this sort of material, these sorts of social constructs through intersectional lenses, then I am a great advocate for the use of creative means in order for us to do so.

One of the major reasons for this is that it brings into play the idea of storytelling. All cultures have their own ways of telling stories, from the commodified ways of the Global North where we have books in bookstores by the tens of thousands and we can buy any book at any time, to the oral story tellers of a good number of cultures around the world, be they Aboriginal, Native American, African Caribbean, or South Asian. Storytelling as a part of the creative techniques walks hand in hand with the creative imagery displayed and explored previously in this book, because in both Chapter 4 and Chapter 5 there are attempts by the psyche to tell a story which is then heard by the conscious mind.

These stories are made sense of by the client themselves. Sometimes with the help of the therapist, but not always, and the importance of these is that even this methodology, even these ways of working, even these ways of bringing understanding stretch us beyond those colonised ways of working and being with clients when we talk about race, racism, and racial constructions.

References

Alonso, A., & Rutan, J. S. (1988). Shame and guilt in psychotherapy supervision. *Psychotherapy*, *25*(4), 576–581.

Andersson, J. (2020). Channel 4's controversial Dispatches Gypsy documentary 'has set the community back by decades', campaigners say. INews.Co.Uk. https://inews.co.uk/news/channel-4-dispatches-gypsy-documentary-has-set-community-back-decades-campaigners-419356

Arendt, H. (2022). *Eichmann in Jerusalem: A report on the banality of evil*. Penguin Classics.

Bauman, W. A. (2023). Indigenous methodologies, decolonizing the academy, and reconnecting stories with planetary places. *Religious Studies Review*, *49*(2), 165–167. https://doi.org/10.1111/rsr.16544

Benjamin, J. (1998). *Shadow of the other*. Routledge.

Benjamin, S., & Dillette, A. K. (2021). Black travel movement: Systemic racism informing tourism. *Annals of Tourism Research*, *88*, 103169. https://doi.org/10.1016/j.annals.2021.103169

Besser, A., & Priel, B. (2010). Grandiose narcissism versus vulnerable narcissism in threatening situations: Emotional reactions to achievement failure and interpersonal rejection. *Journal of Social and Clinical Psychology*, *29*(8), 874–902. https://doi.org/10.1521/jscp.2010.29.8.874

Boffey, D. (2018, November). Empire 2.0: the fantasy that's fuelling Tory divisions on Brexit. *Guardian Online*, 1. www.theguardian.com/politics/2018/nov/08/empire-fantasy-fuelling-tory-divisions-on-brexit

Boyz, H. D. and the. (2002). *Heavy D: 20th Century Masters. Millennium Edition*. MCA Records.

Brewster, F. (2020). *The racial complex: A Jungian perspective on culture and race*. Routledge.

Brewster, F. (2023). *Race and the unconscious: An Africanist depth psychology perspective on dreaming*. Routledge.

Clement, J. (2014). *Widow Basquiat*. Canongate Books.

Cooke, S. (2016). *A Change Gonna Come*. Portrait of a Legend (1951–1964). www.youtube.com/watch?v=wEBlaMOmKV4

Diangelo, R. (2018). *White fragility: Why it's so hard for white people to talk about racism*. Beacon Press.

Dubois, W. E. B. (2023). *The W.E.B. Dubois collection*. Grapevine India.

Egilmez, O. B., & Orum, M. H. (2018). Intercourse type of situational anejaculation or inability to ejaculate intra-vaginally: Three case reports from a conservative Islamic community. *Psychiatry and Clinical Psychopharmacology*, *28*(4), 473–476. https://doi.org/10.1080/24750573.2018.1468618

Ellis, E. (2021). *The Race conversation: An essential guide to creating life-changing dialogue*. Confer Books.

Fanon, F. (2005). *Black skin, white mask* (M. Silverman (ed.)). Manchester University Press.

Flynn, J. E. (2015). White fatigue: Naming the challenge in moving from an individual to a systemic understanding of racism. *Multicultural Perspectives, 17*(3). https://doi.org/10.1 080/15210960.2015.1048341

Haider, S. (2016). The shooting in Orlando, terrorism or toxic masculinity (or both?). *Men and Masculinities, 19*(5), 555–565. https://doi.org/10.1177/1097184X16664952

Hall, S. (1996). *Critical dialogues in cultural studies*. Routledge.

Hall, S. (1997). Who needs identity. *The British Journal of Sociology, 48*(1), 208. https://doi.org/10.2307/591920

Hegel, G. (1976). *Phenomenology of spirit*. Oxford University Press.

Hooks, B. (2016). Feminism is for everybody. In *Ideals and ideologies: A reader*. https://doi.org/10.4324/9781315625546

Hunt, I. M., Richards, N., Bhui, K., Ibrahim, S., Turnbull, P., Halvorsrud, K., Saini, P., Kitson, S., Shaw, J., Appleby, L., & Kapur, N. (2021). Suicide rates by ethnic group among patients in contact with mental health services: An observational cohort study in England and Wales. *The Lancet. Psychiatry, 8*(12), 1083–1093. https://doi.org/10.1016/S2215-0366(21)00354-0

Hyams, P. (1978). *Capricorn One* (p. 1). Warner Bros. https://www.imdb.com/find/?q=capricorn one&ref_=nv_sr_sm

Kindig, J. (2015). *Selma, Alabama (Bloody Sunday, March 7, 1965)*. Blackpast.Org. www.blackpast.org/aah/bloody-sunday-selma-alabama-march-7-1965

Krizan, Z., & Johar, O. (2012). Envy divides the two faces of narcissism. *Journal of Personality, 80*(5), 1415–1451. https://doi.org/10.1111/j.1467-6494.2012.00767.x

Lick, D. J., Durso, L. E., & Johnson, K. L. (2013). Minority stress and physical health among sexual minorities. *Perspectives on Psychological Science, 8*(5), 521–548. https://doi.org/10.1177/1745691613497965

Marlan, S. (2005). *The black sun: The alchemy and art of darkness*. Texas A&M University Press.

Memmi, A. (1974). *The colonizer and the colonized*. Souvenir Press.

Mereish, E. H. (2012). The intersectional invisibility of race and disability status: An exploratory study of health and discrimination facing Asian Americans with disabilities. *Ethnicity and Inequalities in Social Care, 5*(2), 52–60. https://doi.org/10.1108/17570981211286796

Michallon, C. (2019). John Wayne lays out racist, homophobic views in resurfaced Playboy interview: 'I believe in white supremacy.' *Independent Online*. www.independent.co.uk/arts-entertainment/films/news/john-wayne-playboy-interview-1971-racist-homophobic-white-supremacy-a8788456.html

Mitchell, J. (1986). *The selected Melanie Klein*. Penguin.

O'Connor, S. (2022). *Sinead O'Connor: Rememberings*. Penguin.

Ogden, T. H. (1979). On projective identification. *International Journal of Psycho-Analysis, 60*, 357–373.

Perera, S. B. (1986). *The scapegoat complex: Toward a mythology of shadow and guilt*. Inner City Books.

Peters, C. (2018). *Black music in Europe: A hidden history*. BBC Sounds. www.bbc.co.uk/sounds/play/b09l02hv

Proctor, J. (2004). *Stuart Hall: Routledge critical thinkers*. Routledge.

Rachel, D. (2024). *Too much, too young: The 2 tone records story*. White Rabbit.

Samuels, A. (1994). Jung and antisemitism. *The Jewish Quarterly, 1*, 12–15.

Schamp, J. (2016). Creolizing Jung: Re-imagined alchemy and individuation in Anton Nimblett's *Sections of an Orange* and Lelawattee Manoo-Rahming's *Curry Flavour*. *Journal of Postcolonial Writing, 9855*(February), 1–14. https://doi.org/10.1080/174498 55.2015.1127280

Schubert, M. (n.d.). *The 'German nation' and the 'black Other': Social Darwinism and the cultural mission in German colonial discourse*. https://doi.org/10.1080/0031322X.2011.624754

Simone, N. (1966). *Wild is the Wind*. Verve Records.

Spielberg, S. (1993). *Schindler's List*. Universal Pictures.

Stein, M. (2005). Individuation: Inner work. *Journal of Jungian Theory and Practice*, *7*(2), 1–13.

Thomas, L. K. (2013). Empires of mind: Colonial history and its implications for counselling and psychotherapy. *Psychodynamic Practice*, *19*(2), 117–128. https://doi.org/10.1080/14753634.2013.778484

Troya, M. I., Spittal, M. J., Pendrous, R., Crowley, G., Gorton, H. C., Russell, K., Byrne, S., Musgrove, R., Hannah-Swain, S., Kapur, N., & Knipe, D. (2022). Suicide rates amongst individuals from ethnic minority backgrounds: A systematic review and meta-analysis. *EClinicalMedicine*, *47*, 101399. https://doi.org/10.1016/j.eclinm.2022.101399

Turner, D. D. L. (2021). *Intersections of privilege and otherness in counselling and psychotherapy* (1st ed.). Routledge.

Turner, D. D. L. (2022). *Decolonise Me IV: From the exotification to the humanity of Black masculinity*. Dwight Turner Counselling. www.dwightturnercounselling.co.uk/2022/12/15/decolonise-me-iii-from-the-exotification-to-the-humanity-of-black-masculinity/

Tyagi, A. (2008). Individuation : The Jungian process of spiritual growth. *Explorations of Human Spirituality*, 128–153.

Various. (1965). *Til Death Do Us Part*. BBC.

Various. (1996). *Goodness Gracious Me*. BBC. www.bbc.co.uk/iplayer/episodes/b007xm15/goodness-gracious-me

Various. (2018). 'Star Trek's' interracial kiss 50 years ago boldly went where none had gone before. NBC News. www.nbcnews.com/news/nbcblk/star-trek-s-interracial-kiss-50-years-ago-went-boldly-n941181

Various. (2020). George Floyd Death. BBC News. www.bbc.co.uk/news/topics/cv7wlylxzg1t/george-floyd-death

Various. (2021). U.S. Capitol Riot. *The New York Times*. www.nytimes.com/spotlight/us-capitol-riots-investigations

Various. (2023a). The Genesis of *Doctor Who*. BBC Online. https://www.bbc.co.uk/articles/cx8rvvrej7zo

Various. (2023b). *Therapists challenging racism and oppression* (N. Zahid & R. Cooke (eds.)). PCCS Books.

Williams, W. (2020). *Windrush Lessons Learned Review* (Issue March). www.gov.uk/government/publications/windrush-lessons-learned-review

Yunkaporta, T. (2024). *Sand talk: How Indigenous thinking can save the world*. Text Publishing.

Chapter 6

Conclusion

Introduction

In April 2024 Channel 4 broadcast the programme *Defiance* (Ahmed, 2024), a series of three documentaries, created by the South Asian artist and actor Riz Ahmed. These documentaries highlighted the struggles of South Asian families who had come to the United Kingdom in the 1960s and 1970s and settled in areas such as Southall, Brick Lane, Rochdale, and other areas of the United Kingdom. The struggles were, of course, based around their racial difference, with the 1970s being a time when South Asians endured a lot of hatred from the working class British, nay English persons who lived in those areas originally, a hatred fuelled by the speeches of people such as Enoch Powell and his 'Rivers of Blood' speech (Sandbrook, 2023).

The importance of a documentary like this is that it brings back to the surface many of the stories and the narratives of a time which, for many of us outside of the South Asian community, seems to have become lost in the fogginess of our racial history. So that whilst we understand and know and empathise with the deaths of Damilola Taylor, Stephen Lawrence, and other Black individuals, the names of South Asian men and boys, who also lost their lives, have sadly become lost along the way (Myers & Bhopal, 2015). It is important to remember the names of Gurdip Singh Chaggar (and the later murder of the teacher Blair Peach) because it brings back to the surface one or the core aspects of this book, the idea that racism and racial hatred are not just relegated to Black and white (Sharma, 2019). This is the importance of a book such as this – or rather, this is one of the key areas. The fact that racism continues is because we all have an identity staked within a racialised sense of who we are; be it because we wish it to be so, or because it has been placed upon us from without, in the Global North we all have a racialised identity.

The second part of this is to bring back to the fore the idea of struggle – the struggles for survival as I have just hinted at; the struggles for survival in an environment which wants to annihilate the racialised other. The trauma of the South Asian community, as so eloquently and beautifully presented in the programme *Defiance*, speaks a great deal and holds massive echoes of the trauma explored in Chapter 3

DOI: 10.4324/9781003508854-6

within this book (Ahmed, 2024), because race as an identity is socially constructed and because it is not a natural, fluid, elegant form of identity.

That lived experience of the hatred of the National Front in the 1970s would have been incredibly traumatic for a generation of migrants who had come to the United Kingdom believing that they were British because their parents had been born and raised within the era of colonialism. To have that sense of hatred reinforced by the far right and also underpinned by structures such as the police or the government would have been a huge shock to the South Asian cultural system. That this happens not just to South Asians or other groups is undeniable, but I will add that it probably happens in slightly separate ways, depending on which group one belongs to. The important point to recognise though, is that for this particular culture the trauma of trying to find a way of surviving also meant that they bonded together, came close together, and the community became tighter in its own way.

I was born and raised in West London in Hammersmith, and went to school in the area with a sizeable number of children from South Asian backgrounds whose parents had worked incredibly hard to send them to the same school that I went to. A respectable number of people that I met and studied alongside from the South Asian community are friends of mine now, and I know and remember Southall, for example, really well. And yet, given the times dictated within a programme such as *Defiance*, even I had started to forget. There is something about the myopia of one's own struggles that can often lead us, in my experience, to reject, forget, or ignore that there are other racialised struggles going on all around us.

The next important thing about a book like this is that it has taken a phenomenological approach to identity, race, and racism. What I have done, I believe, is show that, in the '*siloisation*' of our individualised racial struggles, we re-enact one of racism's core tricks. What this does in many ways is to make us believe that our experience is an isolated experience, it is a one-off – and yet, what often gets called out later time and time again, is that actually racism is systemic, is institutional. This book aims to provide evidence of that by presenting numerous experiences, interactions, and endurances around race and racism for many diverse groups and the collective stories presented in this text highlight how racism is not just an individual experience. Racialised hatred is not just a one-off, it is something which is the core fabric of the world that we live within and the intersectional, racialised identity that we all have to embody in the Global North.

This is why when people say we must dismantle and challenge racism, it is incredibly difficult, if not close to impossible, to do so. Race as a construct built out of whiteness and built out of the superiority of an English or European upper class, has become so self-functioning and self-replicating, that to disrupt or to destroy it is, I believe, impossible. We have an identity which has been placed upon us that we have to learn to live with and, I will argue here, live beyond, and this is where counselling and psychotherapy can play a huge role.

This is why, whenever we see things moving, progressing one or two steps forward to borrow a Hegelian perspective on culture and difference, what we also have to recognise is actually that these things, these changes, be they incremental and slow, often revert back to type (Hegel, 1976). The perfect example of this, if you like, could be seen within the rightward shift of cultures across the Global North in this new millennia. Prior to this, there was a lot more hope around race, and difference, and movements forward. Yet, what we have often seen, in the 2020s particularly, is a rightward shift towards populism and a huge fear of the voice and the identity of an awake, racialised other.

I use that phrase 'awake' for a reason because it highlights the idea that, for systemic whiteness, woke culture is something to be feared. Yet, the realism of woke culture, with its origins coming not just from the Bible but from the civil rights activism of generations gone by, is that any attack on wokeism is at its core an attempt by white supremacy to reassert its racialised dominance. So, taking this into the therapy room, for counsellors and psychotherapists who are working with race and racism in the counselling environment, there are three areas that we need to recognise and explore.

The first is the recognition of the racialised identity that we, and our clients, will therefore hold. Be it the therapist or the trainee, someone who identifies as white, and as British, and as male, they will still have a racialised identity which has been passed to them through their own parents, culture, and background. There will be certain ideas about what it is to be white and English, white and Welsh, white and French, white and American, that may have led to their racialised adaptation to fit in with said structures. It could be anything from watching the foods that one eats and rejecting other foods as too ethnic, to noting the music one listens to whilst marginalising music from say Black or Asian cultures as being too ethnic or too aggressive. It can come down to the clothes that one wears or the way that one wears them. There are many ways in which our racialised identity and its connections to culture and the structures of culture then come together.

This will also be the same for the racialised other, just from a different angle – the struggle for many of us who are the racialised other; the acculturated gap between our culture or the culture that marks us out as the racialised other, versus the subject culture and that environment, which wants us to fit in or to become assimilated. Assimilation here is not just something that is used on a base cultural level but, in many different ways, it is something that is advocated for within the political sphere as well (Brubaker, 2001).

Margaret Thatcher, in her comments upon a paper post the Brixton Riots of the 1980s, queried what these riots might have been about because she assumed that minorities who come from the former colonies would by the 1980s have become successfully assimilated into English culture (Unknown, 2014). Her perspective, though, totally ignored two facts: the first being that culture is not a fixed point and two cultures meeting together will often influence each other whether they want that to happen or not; the second is important to recognise – in the elevating of one colonial culture over the other one creates a power dynamic whereby culture and therefore race are hierarchical. So, for Thatcher to assert the idea that those persons who were coming from a different culture need to give up their culture and fit in, was at best naïve and at worst a part of the internalised white supremacy built into the political sphere, which denotes that one culture is more dominant than the other. Yet, although this statement about Thatcher's ideas goes back to the 1980s, we still see similar patterns of the politics of assimilation playing themselves out across other cultures such as within France and the banning of the Burqa (Cohen-Almagor, 2022).

The second aspect for students, therapists, and their clients to start to explore is the recognition and the development of ways of working with the trauma of racism. What I have done with this book is bring to the fore just how deeply seated some of these racist incidents actually run. The idea that we may endure micro-aggressions, that sometimes someone may say something harsh towards us and it has very little to no effect, or that we should just be able to laugh it off, belies the deep psychological harm, nay trauma, that goes with any form of racialised slur.

In our counselling and psychotherapy spaces, it is hugely important for us as practitioners to therefore help clients from across the phenomenological racial spectrum to work through the trauma that they have endured and internalised. The examples that I have given you in this book talk about this trauma perhaps playing itself through such secondary methods as alcoholism, abuse of family and friends, self-isolation, sleep deprivation, and so on. Yet, without a recognition and understanding that these things may well have come up as a part of the endurances of racism, then we miss a huge area of understanding of our clients' underlying experiences.

However, this also has links to further research and ideas. Given that my belief that racism causes a deep, psychological, traumatic shock to our internalised system, developing new ways and/or adapting established ways of working with trauma, I believe is the way forward in broadening out how we work as practitioners. The fact that I work with creative techniques to understand unconscious, internalised experiences, is my way of working, but there are other ways of working with trauma such as Emotional Freedom Technique (EFT) and Eye Movement Desensitisation and Reprocessing (EMDR) which in their own ways work incredibly well with the neurological and therefore physiological impacts of trauma (Various, 2023). These are ways that I believe could be developed and adapted in order for us to work with the traumas that all of our clients experience around race and racism.

In conjunction with this, though, is the work that our courses need to do in exploring the impact of racism upon members of their student cohort. The fact that so many students of colour need to find support outside of their courses because of the systemic racism embedded within the teaching, the methodologies, and the theories, says an awful lot about what they have to endure in order to get on, to get through, and to get out the other end of said training courses. The numerous stories that I have heard over the years of students of colour, of difference, or varying racialised identities, who felt they were unable to bring their racialised identity to a space on their course, experiences which then led to them exploring these things outside, is saddening and sickening in equal measure. This, together with the length of time that these things have been going on for, together with the paucity of change, says an awful lot about the earlier point I made in this chapter – that it is difficult, if not impossible, to disrupt and get rid of racism. That, because it is so self-replicating, it will adapt and play itself out within every single system that we engage with, including our training courses. A way forward for trainees and training courses would therefore involve a greater recognition and also the adapting of a particular space, whereby race and racism becomes a core facet in the explorations of what it is to be white, Black, Asian, Jewish, and so on.

The third factor to recognise here in working with issues of race and racism, is that there needs to be a recognition of how the racialised identity has become adapted to fit into a world of whiteness. This could be for the client with the help of the therapist, but it could also be a part of a course whereby the students themselves have to explore the systemic adaptations they have made in relationship to the super-egoically driven confines of the system's whiteness. What I mean by this is that if we are talking about whiteness as being a driving force, and if we recognise that systemisation does not involve colour, that it is self-replicating, what we start to see is something, a phenomenological experience, which has been internalised by so many of us, whether the racialised other or the racialised subject. The 'Master' and the 'Slave', to use phrases denoted by Fanon and Hagel, are both adapted creatures (Hudis, 2015; Villet, 2011) – the adaptations enforced from without. There is a way that the master must perform in order to be a master. There is a way for the slave to perform in order to be a slave. Systemic whiteness informs both positions.

Within counselling and psychotherapy, helping our clients to recognise the racialised aspects of themselves, which are either master or slave, or – and this is important – aspects which belong to both positions, therefore becomes a core facet of psychotherapy. It could well be that these adaptations are what have led to the systemically driven, unconsciously influencing, silencing that goes with being the racialised other, for example. Or it could be that systemic whiteness is what has driven one to believe that it is OK and good enough to see the racialised other as less than.

However, as I think about this book and construct its narrative, I realise that there is a fourth position to adopt in any sort of exploration of racism and racialised constructs within counselling and psychotherapy. This is to recognise that race in its own way is an incomplete construction. When we factor in how social constructions overlie biological constructions of identity, we have to recognise that, by their very nature, social constructions are a bit like placing a small piece of tracing paper over a large field of grass; they miss, nay ignore the nuances and the vast differences that sit within every aspect of that field, reducing everything down to one or two key blades of grass or core aspects and characteristics. Social constructions of race are in their creation othering of the immensity of the complexity of the biological creation.

Because our identities have therefore become so reduced within these racialised constructs, to go through a process of individuation, whereby one develops, evolves, and grows beyond said constrictions, therefore means that actually what we try and do in a way is to help our clients come back to who they are as persons of racialised difference. This could be an exploration of what it is to be from a traveller community that involves a client sitting with the ancestral messages, ways, traditions, and understandings so much so that they become more deeply rooted within that particular cultural environment, whilst also perhaps for themselves updating it to a more authentic sense of what systemic subjectivity actually means. What I am saying here is that, as well as developing that cultural side of themselves, the acculturated part of which has imbibed some sort of systemically driven whiteness that has become adapted, this part in its flawed way also needs to change. Both the subject and the other, both the master and the slave, find a unique way of being which fits in with their own individual way of experiencing the world and in that reimagining, that realignment, that reconnecting with past and present, a more authentic way of being comes through.

The racialised cultural aspect therefore evolves. It stretches beyond the stereotypical, performative, and othering confines of what it is to be of colour, South Asian, and so on and it stretches into a more authentic, realistic, and future-facing way of being that involves a deeper connection to self and therefore to others around them. We see this happen a lot within the arts. To return to the origins of say Ska music, whereby the fusion of Reggae with an aspect of punk music then brought with it not only a new type of cultural phenomenon and music, but also connected the working classes of the United Kingdom with the working class of the immigrant populations who arrived in the country as part of the Windrush Generation.

Growth through the individuation away from the oppressive systemic structures of racism is therefore possible, but it takes all of us to reach within ourselves to root out the disease that has been left within us over generations. If we are able to do this then what happens is that we become more than the stereotypes which have been passed through us. We become more than those ways of being which have been defined by whiteness. We become more than the stories which tell us who we are, and through the telling of our own stories we start to develop new ways of relating, of telling our own modern-day tales of who we are and who we wish to be.

To end this book, though, as stated in the prologue to this text, one of the most difficult things about writing a book about race and racism was always going to be the fact that I would be telling and utilising not just my own stories, but the stories of my compatriots on these pages. These stories were always going to become the touchstones of hatred from those who are so much in denial of the idea of racism and so afraid that they may too have been co-opted into an idea of what it is to be white and English, white and American, white and European. I could have put white in all these instances in brackets because in their simplistic way of seeing difference and diversity, what even they failed to recognise in not seeing whiteness as more than just colour, is that they too are wrapped up in a way of being which is not their own. They have bought into the idea that they are superior because of a simple thing like the colour of their skin.

From Presidents of America to members of the National Front and other fascist groups, even members of the differing political parties in the United Kingdom (including the political left!), these ideas and structures about the certain value that we are supposed to have because we are English and white, or that we are English and football fans, or whatever this might be, take away from and distort the fact that, actually, difference and diversity in its richness brings so much more to our countries, to our cultures, to aspects of our lives than we can ever truly understand. From the adoption of forms of music, to the incorporation of traditional dishes into our cuisine, to the winners of baking programmes on national television, the development and envelopment of the racialised other into what is Britishness, nay Englishness, no whiteness, will continue ad infinitum even should so many others in positions of power, and not, wish it otherwise.

Books like this, therefore, have a huge role to play in understanding the silent voices of the racialised other and challenging the systemic structures which create said invisibility and superiority. So, the more that we look to stretch beyond the ways that we have been told to be, the more likely it is that we will actually start to find peace and harmony.

Recognising the humanity of the other is what sits on these pages. Telling my own stories, for example, is not based upon some sort of narcissistic need to bare my soul. It is actually based upon the fact that as a human being I invite the reader, the other, and the subject to see me as a human being. I invite them to look beyond whatever guilt and shame they may experience when they hear, read, or feel my stories and I invite them to not so much feel bad about anything that has happened to myself because that is not what it is about, but to recognise that actually in order for us to all work together and be together, one has to reach a space of racialised and cultural humility.

This is the same for any of us, myself included. When I encounter aspects of difference that I have not met before, my sometimes struggle but oftentimes willingness to meet the other where they happen to be, involves me coming down from whatever self-perceived step of superiority I may have placed myself upon, to sit down on the ground with that other and hear what they have to say to me. Yet, too often in the world of counselling and psychotherapy I come across counsellors and psychotherapists for whom this seems like the trickiest thing to do.

So, my final call to all who read this text is as follows: read it, learn from it, and move on from it. Build structures around it, tell your own stories. I want to hear them. We need to hear them. They should be heard. Only then does this rich phenomenological tapestry then really become what I hope it will do. A blanket which, when revealed, when seen, when experienced, and when felt, touches all of us.

References

Ahmed, R. (2024). *Defiance: Fighting the Far Right*. Rogan Productions, Channel 4. https://roganproductions.co.uk/project/defiance-fighting-the-far-right/

Brubaker, R. (2001). The return of assimilation? Changing perspectives on immigration and its sequels in France, Germany, and the United States. *Ethnic and Racial Studies, 24*(4), 531–548. https://doi.org/10.1080/0141987012004977

Cohen-Almagor, R. (2022). Indivisibilité, sécurité, laïcité: The French ban on the burqa and the niqab. *French Politics, 20*(1), 3–24. https://doi.org/10.1057/s41253-021-00164-8

Hegel, G. (1976). *Phenomenology of spirit*. Oxford University Press.

Hudis, P. (2015). Frantz Fanon's contribution to Hegelian Marxism. *Critical Sociology*, 1–9. https://doi.org/10.1177/0896920515610894

Myers, M., & Bhopal, K. (2015). Racism and bullying in rural primary schools: Protecting White identities post Macpherson. *British Journal of Sociology of Education*, *5692* (October), 1–19. https://doi.org/10.1080/01425692.2015.1073099

Sandbrook, D. (2023). *Enoch Powell's 'Rivers of Blood' speech: Britain and race in the mid 20th-century*. History Extra: The Official Website for *BBC History Magazine*. www.historyextra.com/period/20th-century/enoch-powell-rivers-blood-speech-what/

Sharma, G. (2019). The British Asians who fought fascism in the seventies. Aljazeera. *https://*www.aljazeera.com/features/2019/4/23/the-british-asians-who-fought-fascism-in-the-seventies

Unknown. (2014). Margaret Thatcher's criticism of Brixton riot response revealed. BBC website. www.bbc.co.uk/news/uk-30600064

Various. (2023). *EMDRWorks*. https://emdrworks.org/costs/

Villet, C. (2011). Hegel and Fanon on the question of mutual recognition: A comparative analysis. *The Journal of Pan African Studies*, *4*(7), 39–51.

Index

Aboriginal, 56, 66, 90, 117
Aboud, 44, 49–51, 53, 65
Adverse Childhood Experience (ACE), 55, 67
African, 7, 24, 34, 39, 44, 66, 74, 89, 92, 117, 127
Akbar, 33, 37, 45, 65, 71–72, 88
allyship, 93
American, 14, 16–17, 24, 38, 40, 48, 65, 68, 74, 89, 96, 99, 109, 117–118, 122, 125
antisemitism, 13, 16, 26, 39, 45–46, 66, 99, 118
Arendt, 94, 117

Baldwin, ix–x
Blackness, 3–4, 6, 13–14, 24, 31, 33, 47, 59
bodywork, 72, 74–75
Brewster, 100, 105, 109, 117

Caribbean, 3, 8, 15, 17–19, 24, 31–32, 37, 59, 65, 96, 102–103, 117
Celtic, 12, 92, 103
China, 14
classism, 15, 23, 36, 38
climate change, 36, 38, 40
code switching, 26–27, 33, 38, 47, 51, 54, 84, 103, 106, 108
cognitive, 7, 11, 20, 69, 71, 75, 107, 116
colonialism, 5, 7, 13, 18, 23–24, 30, 32–33, 36, 38–41, 52, 67, 98, 121

Diangelo, 6, 16, 48, 65, 102, 117
dreams, 6, 100, 105, 108–109, 112, 114
dreamwork, 51
Dubois, 93, 117

Ellis, 2, 16, 21, 38, 102, 118
embodiment, 59
EMDR (Eye Movement Desensitisation and Reprocessing), 58, 123
envy, 43, 45–47, 49, 96, 99, 108, 118
exotification, 32–33, 38, 119

Fanon, 48, 66, 99–100, 118, 124, 127
fatphobia, 29, 33, 43, 71
First Nations, 16–17, 24
Freud, 16–17, 39

George Floyd, 2–3, 17, 23–24, 27, 41, 68, 90–91, 114, 119
guilt, 93–96, 99, 110, 114, 117–118, 126

Hall, 48
hate, ix, 8, 24, 37–38, 45–47, 54, 65–66, 86, 96, 99, 107
Hegel, 20, 39, 48, 66, 100–101, 110, 118, 122, 127
historical erasure, 30, 38–39, 43

India, 35–37, 39, 117
Indigenous, 14, 16, 89–90, 92, 96, 104, 117, 119
individuation, 21, 40, 95, 99–105, 118–119, 124–125
institutional, 9–10, 23–24, 27, 34–35, 60–62, 68, 121
internalised racism, 11, 15, 23, 31, 65, 88, 108–109, 115
interpersonal, 9, 11, 19–20, 23–24, 27, 30, 62, 105, 117
intersectionality, 15, 39
islamophobia, 13, 46

Jewish, viii, 7, 11, 13, 27–28, 30, 37, 43–44, 48, 54, 66, 79, 82, 86, 97, 111, 118, 124
John Paul Sartre, 4
Jung, 21, 39, 89, 99, 118

Kinouani, 2, 16, 21, 39
Klein, 45, 48, 65–66, 118

Levinas, 20, 39
Levine, 73, 89
Lorde, x

Maori, 7
Memmi, 100, 118
Merleau-Ponty, 8, 16–17, 20, 40, 71, 84–85, 89
mimicry, 23, 51, 67

Native American, 14, 16, 74, 89, 117
neurological, 43, 56–59, 61, 63, 65, 68, 86, 105, 123

Ogden, 73, 89, 94, 118

patriarchy, 5, 7, 12–13, 21, 23, 29, 36–37, 44, 95–97
phenomenology, 2, 4, 6–8, 10, 12, 14–16, 18–41, 44, 46, 48, 50, 52, 54, 56, 58, 60, 62, 64, 66, 70–74, 76, 78, 80, 82, 84, 86, 88–89, 92, 94–96, 98, 100, 102, 104, 106, 108, 110, 112, 114, 116, 118, 122, 124, 126–127
physical health, 16, 58, 118
Piaget, 44, 67
politics, 17, 19, 46, 55, 66–67, 91, 117, 123, 126
populism, 48, 66, 103, 122

race, 3–7, 9–10, 12, 14–17, 19–22, 25, 32, 37–38, 40–41, 43–50, 55–56, 59, 61, 65–66, 68–72, 85, 87, 89, 91–93, 95–100, 102, 104–107, 115–118, 121–125, 127; race science, 17, 22, 40
racial displacement, 31
racial historical erasure, 30
racial homophobia, 30
racial invisibility, 25–26
racial othering, 84, 92
racial performance anxiety, 25, 86
racial performativity, 25
racial punching down, 31

racial realignment, 94–95
racial victim blaming, 27–28
Rogers, 89
Roma, 13, 15–16, 37, 52, 65, 67
Romany, viii, 7, 52, 54, 75, 91, 103

Saini, 10, 17, 35, 40, 66, 118
Samaritans, 62, 67
self-hatred, 31, 47, 94, 99
shame, ix, 23, 25, 36–37, 41, 46–47, 51, 53, 55, 59, 72, 86, 93–94, 96, 99, 103, 110, 117, 126
silencing, ix–x, 6, 13, 21, 47, 109, 111, 113, 124
somatic, 11, 69–70, 72–74, 84, 87
South American, 14
South Asian, 7, 13, 48, 54, 63, 91, 97–98, 103, 117, 120–121, 125
splitting, 7–8, 10, 25, 48, 68, 71–72, 76, 84, 86–87, 91, 100, 102, 115
stereotyping, 47, 71, 98, 103
supremacy, x, 2, 5, 7, 13–14, 17, 19, 21, 23, 28–30, 33, 36–37, 39–40, 44, 55–56, 96–97, 118, 122
systemic, ix–x, 4–5, 7, 9–12, 14, 22–24, 27, 29–30, 34–35, 37–38, 43–44, 46–50, 54–57, 60–62, 68, 73, 75, 92–96, 98–99, 101, 103–105, 108–110, 115–118, 121–126

Thingification, 33
trauma, 8, 11, 16–17, 37, 39–40, 42–43, 45, 47, 49, 51, 53, 55–59, 61–65, 67–69, 71, 73–75, 84, 89, 116, 120–121, 123

unconscious racism, 9

van der Kolk, 8, 17, 73, 89
von Franz, 73, 86, 89

white supremacy, 2, 5, 7, 14, 17, 19, 21, 23, 28, 30, 36–37, 44, 55–56, 96–97, 118, 122
whiteness, ix–x, 4–7, 12–14, 19, 22–23, 25, 31–33, 35, 37–38, 45, 47, 49–50, 55, 92, 95–98, 101–105, 107, 109, 112–114, 121–122, 124–126
whitesplaining, 28–29
Windrush, 18, 26, 32, 102, 119, 125

Yunkaporta, 90, 119

For Product Safety Concerns and Information please contact our EU
representative GPSR@taylorandfrancis.com
Taylor & Francis Verlag GmbH, Kaufingerstraße 24, 80331 München, Germany

www.ingramcontent.com/pod-product-compliance
Lightning Source LLC
Chambersburg PA
CBHW050615280326
41932CB00016B/3054